DOREEN McBRIDE
WE ARE OUR PAST

GW00598392

POOLBEG

First published by Adare Press 1990
with grant-aid from the Cultural Traditions Group, Northern Ireland
This revised edition published 1992 by
Poolbeg Press Ltd
Knocksedan House,
Swords, Co Dublin, Ireland

ISBN 1 85371 191 8

A catalogue record for this book is available from the British Library

Cover design by Pomphrey Associates
Illustrations and photographs by the author unless otherwise specified
Set by Richard Parfrey in ITC Stone Serif 10/14
Printed by The Guernsey Press Company Ltd,
Vale, Guernsey, Channel Islands

Acknowledgements

It is always pleasant to remember the many people who so generously gave help. Sincere thanks are due to the staff of the Ulster Folk and Transport Museum: Bill Crawford, Linda Ballard, Philip Robinson, Deirdre Brown, Andrew Anderson, Deborah McAuley, Jonathan Bell, Mervyn Watson, Ken Anderson and Michael Donnelly.

I am also indebted to Dara Vallelly, the Armagh Rhymers; John Gilmore and Evelyn Cardwell, The Ulster American Folk Park; Tony Canavan, The Federation of Ulster Local Studies; Valerie Hall, Institute of Irish Studies, Queen's University Belfast; Jean Kelly, Benburb Centre; Tom Collins, Dungannon Multi-purpose Centre; Elizabeth McWaters, University Bookshop; Alwyn Corrin, Fairfields Bookshop; Anne Tannahill, Blackstaff Press.

Hal Crowe, editor of *Farm Week*, provided valuable information as did Colm Barton and Deirdre McNully, Southern Education and Library Board; Elizabeth Harkin, The History Park, County Tyrone; Brian Lambkin; Heather Crawford; Frances Shaw; Charles McCourt; Ernest Scott; Nigel Jess; Di Watson; George Bryson; Lil McCusker; Jim Holland; Cahal Dallat; Roy Hamilton; Noelle and Graham Millar; Robert Bell; Maureen Armstrong and Marie Ward.

Thanks are due to my husband, George, Pat Meads and Lance Macmanaway, who edited the original text.

My daughter, Leona, and son, John, gave unlimited support. I am grateful to them.

I am indebted to Margaret and Robert Boston for permission to photograph their home, Laurelvale and to the Ulster American Folk Park for permission to reproduce a photograph of their replica of an emigrant ship.

Contents

"You may not realise it, but the blood of saints and scholars
runs in my veins."

1

We Are Our Past

This book is an exploration of my past, aspects of which are shared by everyone of Irish descent. It includes things I have seen and heard, the memories of people I know, people from every walk of life and all sides of the community and the places involved.

There have been more changes in the past hundred years than there have been in the previous thousand. If Rip Van Winkle had gone to sleep in 1890 and wakened up in 1990 think of his surprise and perhaps his horror: aeroplanes, motorcars, electric light, fires and stoves, washing machines, tumble dryers, radio and television. Think of the way the landscape has changed, the change in house types, to say nothing of central heating, modern plumbing, modern sewage works, hospitals, modern medicine and good water supplies piped into buildings.

I remember my grandmother sitting by the fire talking to my mother. "It is a poor summer," she said. "Hunger will stalk the land." At the time I thought that was just granny's old-fashioned talk and dismissed it. Now I am not so sure. I feel we have a lot to be thankful for. Today in Ireland, very few people face the prospect of starving to death. It is a sobering thought that in Belfast and

Dublin in the 1850s the average expectancy of life was twenty-nine years. Life expectancy throughout Europe was low, until people were provided with safe water supplies and efficient means of sewage disposal.

Estyn Evans was a much-loved Professor of Geography at Queen's University, Belfast. He suggested that each person has folk memories, unconscious feelings that have been passed down from generation to generation. It may

Old fireplace adapted for use today

Laurelvale, Moy, County Tyrone

be fanciful, but I believe it to be true. I feel extra satisfaction as I tend my fire, that old-fashioned source of heat and comfort much loved by Irish people, realising that I am responding to a distant folk memory of days and nights spent around the fire enjoying "good crack*."

I was intrigued by the reactions of some Americans of Irish descent to my fire. They loved it! They sat up close saying they could imagine their ancestors sitting around a fire such as that in the past. Perhaps Irish folk memories are present in all the corners of the world containing Irish emigrants? At any rate, it is true to say that each individual is under the influence of his, or her, past. The past includes half-forgotten memories of childhood and the family's oral history, which shapes attitudes, even if unconsciously. To a large extent we are our past.

* "crack" means conversation in Ireland

2

Home, Sweet Home

Like the majority of people, my attitudes were formed at home. Evenings sitting around the ever-important fire left a lasting impression. The atmosphere created by the flickering flames is entirely absent from our, admittedly more comfortable, centrally heated homes. The Irish are a nation of home-lovers and it is interesting to see how these homes have changed over the centuries. In Ireland the earliest homes were round or rectangular structures. Many homes were sited on crannógs—artificial islands built in lakes. Many crannógs had underwater "causeways" made from woven reeds. These causeways were held in position by wooden pegs which looked like modern tent pegs. People living on the crannóg knew where the causeway was situated. They escaped from enemies by running across the causeway, then pulling it behind them. Crannógs were used from about 1200 BC to AD 1700.

These early houses were made on a wooden frame with a closely woven wickerwork of hazel or birch. Two walls were built in close proximity, the space between the walls filled with heather as insulation, the spaces in the wickerwork with mud and daub.

Crannóg, Loughbrickland, County Down

Reconstruction of a crannóg, History Park, Gortín, County Tyrone

The fireplace was important in the earliest houses. If the mud fell off the walls the wooden frame was uncovered and could catch fire; so the fireplace was set in the middle of the building, with a hole in the roof above it to let the smoke out. Round houses had the highest point of the roof in the centre of the building. Rectangular houses had a central ridgepole running along the length of the house so that the highest point of the roof was also in the centre. A central fire, with the highest point of the roof above it, was less likely to burn the house down than one set against a wall.

A central hearth had other advantages. It warmed the whole house, not just one corner. People could sit in a circle around it and each person had a fair share of the heat. During dark winter evenings people could gather together and indulge in "crack," that is, conversation, something which Irish people love. People also told stories at the fireside and this led to Ireland's rich tradition of story-telling. At the end of an evening's crack people slept in a circle on the bare floor around the fire with their feet pointing towards it.

There used to be a railway station at Ashfield, near Dromore in County Down. It had a fire in the centre of its waiting room. Old age pensioners from the district recall the crack around that particular fire. During the winter time people used to come from miles away to sit around the fire and chat. Apparently most of them had no intention of going anywhere. They just enjoyed the company in the railway station with its central fire and the age-old social pattern.

Chimneyless houses must have been full of smoke. Look at the following description of a house that belonged to the Irish hero called Gillo.

And when the occasion did require
In midst of house a mighty fire
Of black dry'd earth and swinging blocks,
Was made enough to roast an ox,
From which arose such clouds of smoak,
As either you or me would choak,
But Gillo and his train inur'd
To smoak, the same with ease endur'd,
By sitting low on rushes spread,
The smoak still hover'd overhead,
And did more good than real harm,
Because it kept the long house warme
And never made their heads to ake,
Therefore no chimney he would make
And thus for smoak altho' 'twas dear,
He paid four shillings every year.

Gillo paid four shillings every year for his smoke because in 1662 the Hearth Money Act was passed. He must have had two chimneys because the Hearth Money Act was a house tax rather than a poll tax. It placed a tax of two shillings on every hearth, fireplace or stove in all houses which had an annual valuation of more than eight shillings. It was said that the Irish were willing to pay extra for smoke because they thought "it nourisheth and keepeth warme their children." Chimney smoke was believed to be beneficial until well into the twentieth century.

In July 1963, I remember, I visited Grace Kerr, an old lady who lived in Ahoghill, County Antrim. She was a great old lady, well into her eighties, who lived in a tiny, traditional house untouched by any attempt at modernisation. She bade us welcome and drew "creepie" stools up to the fire to make us comfortable. The fireplace was set in the wall furthest from the door and at right-angles to it. It had an open hearth and a crook on which pots and kettles were hung. Grace arranged the kettle on the crook and swung it over the fire asking us if we would like a cup of tea. As I drank my tea, I gazed up the chimney at the sky and began to cough and splutter because of the dense smoke inside the house. Grace and other locals who had come in for a chat laughed at my discomfort saying, "Townies are all the same. They can't stand a drop of smoke," and "Smoke is good for you. Do you not know it is very nourishing?" Later I was mortified to overhear two elderly gentlemen discussing me. "That wee girl," they said, "will not make much of a wife. She's too small and not broad enough to be able to pull a plough. And did you hear her cough? She'll catch TB and die young, I'm telling you. She's useless!"

Although Grace was old, her house was tidy and well ordered. She had the traditional buckets of water standing inside the door. She explained that it was unlucky to go to bed at night without making sure that there was plenty of water stored for the next day. Grace told me she washed her feet very carefully before going to bed at night. She said it was unlucky not to throw out water in which feet had been washed. It was possible to share foot water provided that after each person had finished using the water in turn, a piece of hot coal from the fire was picked up with the fire tongs and dropped in the water. Grace told me she was always careful to empty it into the drain outside. She never simply threw it outside the door because that could annoy the fairies and bring bad luck.

Keeping clean was a real problem without a supply of running water. Water had to be carried from the well in buckets which were usually left standing inside the door of the house, beside the wall. This water was carefully hoarded and used several times. Water in which potatoes had been boiled was saved and used to wash dishes, hands or clothes before being thrown out.

Saturday night was traditionally "bath night." A zinc bath, or a waterproof wooden tub, was pulled out in front of the fire, filled with water heated in kettles over the fire, and used by each member of the family. Grace said that in her family the business started with the youngest child and ended with the eldest; each one was washed in turn and put to bed "out of the road." Once the children were finished her mother had her bath, followed by her father. The bath water was saved to wash clothes if it looked at all clean. Grace said, rather sadly, once the water had been used to wash the whole family it was usually very dirty and had to be thrown out. Carrying water was a back-breaking job. There is an old saying in County Tyrone—"She is a great girl. Her back is broad enough to carry two buckets!"

Grace lifted an old framed photograph off the wall to show me. We carried it over to the door to look at it more closely in a good light. It was covered by a thin layer of soot. Grace began to rub the glass with a duster. "It's terrible hard to keep the stour down," she said. I shudder to think what life must have been like inside a house which did not have a chimney.

It is thought that the first chimneys in Ireland were built by monks in the monasteries and by the Anglo-Normans, in their castles such as those at Carrickfergus, Trim and Cahir. It is believed that these early chimneys did not have much impact on the local population because very few people were allowed to visit either a monastery or a castle. Also, it would have been difficult to adapt the idea of a stone chimney built into the wall of a stone house into a structure that was suitable for use in a house with flammable wattle walls and a central hearth.

"Forest" chimneys are believed to be the first kind to have been built into ordinary local homes. They were made in the form of a four-sided funnel, held up by two parallel cross beams, built over the central hearth. They were constructed of lath or wattlework, coated with daub. If the daub fell off the inner surface of the chimney the wooden framework was exposed and it could catch fire. Forest chimneys were very dangerous and houses which had them often burnt down. In time they were replaced by chimneys made of brick or stone. This led to the development of the traditional house type with the fireplace built against an inner wall. Some new houses were built without chimneys up until the end of the nineteenth century.

Sometimes improving landlords caused bad feeling by building chimneys inside tenants' houses. In 1868 Lord Lorton, who had an estate at Rockingham, County Roscommon, decided to improve the houses on his property and so built chimneys. His tenants were furious. They sent a deputation to his lordship asking that the chimneys be destroyed because they made the houses cold. The heat of the fire escaped through the chimney along with the smoke. Chimneys throughout Ireland were blocked up by tenants because they believed the smoke warmed them. On the other hand the unescaping smoke hurt the eyes of women as they cooked over the fire and made their skin resemble smoked ham.

The simplest form of house had one room. The door was placed in the same wall as the window. The chimney

"Would your lordship please remove those newfangled chimneys
and give us back our smoke?"

and hearth could be found in one of two places, either on the wall adjacent to the door or on the opposite wall, that is, on the wall adjacent to the window away from the door. Most houses had only one door.

Houses were built from local materials. The materials used were mud-sods, turf, stone, or clay. The poorest houses were made from sods of mud or sods of turf. They were quick and easy to build. They housed most of the population during the early part of the nineteenth century. At that time the population was still growing rapidly. Smallholdings were divided and subdivided into smaller and smaller fields. Houses had to be built quickly and cheaply. Sods were cut out of the earth or from the bogs in the shape of bricks. The sods were used to build walls and the roof was thatched with materials common locally such as straw or marram grass. Unfortunately sod houses did not have a very long life. Within ten years as a result of rain and damp the walls would begin to bulge and be in danger of falling down, so the occupants propped them up with branches of trees, or anything else that happened to be handy. This type of house practically disappeared when the great famine of the 1840s decimated the population.

Byre houses have also disappeared in Ireland. They used to be common along the whole Atlantic coast of Europe. In a byre dwelling the people lived at one end of the house, the cows at the other. No wall or partition separated the cows from the people. Owning a cow was a sign of wealth, so the byre-house dwellers were comparatively rich.

Cows were tied to posts at one end of the room in the byre house during the winter time. A trench cut into the floor caught their droppings. A hole in the wall of the

house at the bottom of the trench let liquid flow out of the house. This kept the trench from overflowing. People living inside byre houses cleaned them out once a year, removing between ten and twelve tons of manure. This manure was very, very precious because it increased crop yield.

Byre house, Ulster Folk and Transport Museum

A farmer with three acres of land and a cow could feed six people. He would have divided his land into three parts. One part would have been used to grow oats, the second grass and the third potatoes. Crops were rotated each year.

The farmer and his family ate potatoes and oats. They drank the cow's milk. The cow ate grass during the summer and oats during the winter. It produced manure to fertilise the ground. On festive occasions the farmer cut one of the cow's veins and collected blood from it in a bucket. The blood was mixed with oatmeal and used to make black sausages or to give a meaty flavour to stews and soups, providing a delicacy for the occasion.

There is a very interesting tape in the archives of the Ulster Folk and Transport Museum. It was made by an old man who had farmed in County Donegal. He explained on the tape the terrible effect the death of his cow had had on his family. When the cow died it obviously could not produce manure. The family went ahead and planted potatoes without fertilising the soil in the usual way. At harvest time they "dug all day" but found very few potatoes. Normally the family would have been weighed down by the weight of the crop which they would carry home on their backs. Faced with starvation the farmer left his family and travelled to Scotland. He found work and was able to send money home to keep his family from starving and to save up and buy a new cow.

The milk cow was very precious and was treated as one of the family. The fire was believed to give protection from evil spirits so, in a byre house, it was only proper that the cow should have a glimpse of it. Churning was done in front of the fire and the grain was stored inside the house. The single compartment of the byre house acted as byre, living room and granary.

Byre houses were unusual compared to other traditional house types in Ireland. They had two doors, one at the front of the house and the other opposite it at the back. These opposite doors formed a passageway through the house. Cows were usually milked inside the house and the back door allowed them to be driven straight through. Grain was threshed inside the house, just inside the door. This gave rise to the word "threshold." The other door was left open to allow a draught of air to blow the light outer covering, or chaff, of the seeds away.

Byre houses were very unhealthy places in which to live. The occupants were affected by fleas, lice, ticks and other parasites picked up from cows, as well as more serious diseases such as tuberculosis and brucellosis. Needless to say cows also caught these diseases from humans.

Poor people did not have beds. They slept on the bare floor on straw or on a straw-filled bag called a "shake-down." One of my friends remembers a boy who went to the school he attended as a child. The boy was blind in one eye, his pupil completely white because he came from a poor family and slept on straw. A piece of straw had stuck into his eye and blinded him.

Some houses had a half-loft, that is a floor built on top of the walls under the roof space. The half-loft covered about half of the roof space. It was used as a store and the children were lifted up into it to sleep at night. An outshoot, that is a small space about the length and width of a single bed, was frequently built into the wall near the fire, forming a place to sleep. Traditionally old people, or any member of the family who was ill, slept in the bed outshoot because it was warm and snug.

Larger houses had bedrooms. The basic house type was extended in a straight line with the bedroom opening off the main living-room. In some parts of the country it was believed to be unlucky to extend the house on its west side because fairies made paths to the west of human dwellings. Woe betide the inhabitants if they interfered with a fairy path!

Another means of extending a traditional house was to build a second storey on top of the ground floor. This was called "raising the house." If the house was raised the bedrooms were moved upstairs. Corridors did not exist. Rooms simply opened off each other.

Laurelvale, Moy, Co Tyrone. The heart of this house is a single-roomed dwelling with mud walls. It has been extended and "raised."

There was a tax on glass so windows in traditional houses were few and small. This led to the habit of leaving the door open to let light in and to provide ventilation. Traditionally Irish people are very helpful and friendly. An open door was regarded as a sign of welcome although it must have been cold in the winter time. This tradition persists in rural areas today. The door may be shut in deference to modern ideas on central heating but stays unlocked. Visitors are encouraged to open it and walk into the house. In country towns, in spite of advice about the advisability of keeping burglars out, people often leave the key in the lock of the front door so that friends and relations may walk in.

A wide-open door caused draughts, particularly if the fire was adjacent to it. This led to the construction of jam walls. A jam wall was a short wall inside the door. It protected the fire from the draught caused by the open door. Jam walls often had a small window so that the farmer's wife could peep out as she worked at the fire to see who was at the door.

At times an open door was a bit of a nuisance as farm animals and young children could walk in and out at will. This inconvenience led to the invention of the "half-door." The half-door was a door which was cut into two so that the bottom portion could remain shut while the top was opened to give light and ventilation.

According to Irish folklore it is extremely unlucky to destroy an old house because the spirits of the people who lived there in the past would become lost and feel unhappy. Old houses were allowed to decay slowly and only after they were derelict were stones from them used to mend dry-stone walls or for other purposes. Even today Ireland is littered with old houses that are slowly crumbling.

Jam wall inside door

Half-door

Irish folklore also suggests that at night, when the people in the house are asleep, the souls of the old people, that is, the people who lived there in the past, come back. They sit around the fire and contentedly indulge in a bit of crack.

3

The Home, the Hearth and All

The fire warmed the whole house. It also served as a source of heat for cooking, a place to boil the washing, and dry and air clothes, a light source and a focal point for the family and their visitors.

The fire acted as a sign of family continuity because it was never allowed to go out. The housewife tended it last thing at night, pouring ashes over turf embers so that they smouldered quietly until morning when a few rakings with the tongs and the use of bellows brought it to life again. Turf (also called peat) cut from the bogs was the most common fuel. Blocks of wood and coal were used in places where bogs were scarce or supplied poor-quality turf. Coal was used in parts of the east and of the north. It was virtually unknown in the west and the south.

Gorse, also called whin or furze, was sometimes used as a fuel. It burned very quickly and provided good heat. A favourite way to clean a chimney was to drop a rope down it then tie a gorse bush to the end of it. The rope was then pulled up and down the chimney to knock the soot off.

Children collected sticks (*brosna*) used to make the fire light up quickly in the morning. Each child was expected to provide a large bundle and leave it in a basket beside the fire for use the following morning.

Most open hearths had cranes or crooks which were used for cooking. The crane was set in the recess at the left of the fire. Pots were suspended from it on hooks called pot-hangers. The woman of the house was able to swing the crane with its suspended pots over the fire using her left hand. Her right hand was free to stir the contents of the pots. Traditionally the woman sat on the left of the fire so that she was convenient to the crane. The man sat on the right. An old friend, in her ninetieth year, told me that now she loves looking at her hands because they are so clean. In the past, when she cooked over an open fire, her hands became ingrained with soot and always appeared filthy.

It was possible to say how wealthy a household was by looking at the number of cooking pots they owned. The greater the number of cooking pots the wealthier the household. A poor house would have possessed one pot, which would probably have leaked, while a rich house would have owned a whole array of different-sized cooking pots, a kettle and a pot-oven. A pot-oven was a legless pot with a flat lid. A few embers were poked out of the fire on to one side of the hearth. The pot-oven was placed on them and the lid covered with glowing embers. Pot-ovens were used to bake bread. Griddle bread was baked on a griddle, that is a flat round iron plate with a handle to suspend it from the crane. Once the bread was baked it was propped up on a bread stand near the fire to dry out. Bread stands were also used to make toast.

Cooking utensils, Ulster Folk and Transport Museum

Soda bread drying on a bread stand (also called a hamen)

Crickets, insects that look like grasshoppers but bigger, were encouraged to live around the fireplace. A cricket on the hearth was regarded as a sign of good luck. The housewife used a goose wing to spread flour on her griddle before baking potato bread, soda bread, oatcakes and scones. As she spread the flour over the griddle she would flick some on to the hearth to feed the crickets. A good fire, the kettle on the boil and a cricket singing on the hearth represented the soul of comfort and contentment.

I remember as a very young child being taken to visit my mother's old Aunt Bella who lived near Ballynure, in County Down. Aunt Bella was thrilled because a cricket came out and sang on the hearth. I, much to mother's annoyance, burst into tears. I can remember thinking it was a dirty-looking thing and being very upset that it was so near the food I was expected to eat. "Is that cricket not covered in germs?" I sobbed. Aunt Bella laughed and laughed. "That's not a dirty thing like a clock*," she said. "It's very lucky to see a cricket and you should be laughing, not crying; so dry your eyes and stop blubbering!"

The old country kitchen was very different from that found in modern homes. Before the invention of electricity light was at a premium, so the kitchen table was never placed in the centre of the floor. It was set in front of the window so that the farmer's wife would have the greatest amount of light possible as she worked.

Families who lived in single-roomed houses probably did not have a table. They ate around a large cooking pot. Once the potatoes were cooked they were drained through a large strainer made from wickerware and shaped like a

---

* A black beetle. Aunt Bella believed that insects such as house-flies, fleas, cockroaches, etc. which could pass disease to humans were "dirty." All other insects were "clean."

plate with a rim around the edge. The potatoes were placed on the strainer and covered with a clean cloth. The water that was drained off the potatoes was saved and put back in the pot. The steam arising from it kept the potatoes warm. After the meal was finished the water was used to wash the dishes. The family sat around the pot and helped themselves to potatoes. Each member of the family had his or her own special place around the cooking pot. Most families ate out of bowls. These could be filled with soup, or stew, then washed and used for drinking tea.

In Ireland today it is still possible to be invited to "come and have a cup of tea in your hand." This means to have a drink of tea while sitting beside the fire without anyone going to the trouble of laying a formal table.

Rich families had separate dining-rooms and a wealth of china, in contrast to the majority of smallholders who had a single room to serve as a kitchen, a dining-room, a bedroom and a place in which to wash.

The rooms in homes belonging to smallholders tended to be small, so furniture was placed around the walls to avoid cluttering the middle of the floor. Traditionally the dresser was placed against the wall opposite the fire. It was used to display the family's china. Some families had a dresser that held the family china in the top section and hens in the bottom section. A dresser of this type may be seen at Bunratty Folk Park, County Clare.

The fire was the only source of light for poor families. Candles were expensive items. The simplest type of candle was made by dipping rushes in wax. The rush acted as a wick and the wax prevented it from burning too quickly. Sometimes a family would make a pledge to keep a candle lit in the window during the hours of darkness until one of its absent members returned. This represented a

"Come on, on in and I'll give you a wee cup of tea in your hand."

considerable financial sacrifice.

Candles were gradually replaced by oil lamps. Today the majority of houses have electric light. I remember a woman of Gilford, County Down, saying in 1973 that she had recently persuaded her father to put electricity into their farmhouse. She said that she found life was much easier with electric light. She had not realised how much time she had spent preparing the oil lamps for service.

4

Pigs, Hens and Horses

Farmers who were so poor that they could not afford a cow usually had a pig and some hens. These animals were very important because they helped provide the farmer with cash. For this reason the family pig was often called "the gentleman who pays the rent." Pigs are very like humans in many ways. Their skin has a poor covering of hair so they like heat. They appreciate being clean and can be house-trained and so were often treated like family pets.

William Carleton wrote in *Traits and Stories of the Irish Peasantry* about Phil Purcel the pig driver. He described the amazement of a visitor to Phil's father's homestead. They were sitting "cracking" around the fire when an old pig came in through the door, walked over to a ladder that was leaning against the half-loft, climbed it and settled down for a sleep. The father explained that the old pig was very wise and very clean. When it slept, as it often did, near the fire with the occupant of the outshot bed, it always stayed on the side of the bed away from the wall, so if it wanted to go to the toilet in the middle of the night it could get out without disturbing anyone. Apparently that pig had sired many fine piglets and Phil's father expressed the feeling that no one had a greater right in the house than the gentleman who paid the rent.

Phil reared an ancient Irish type of pig that is now extinct. This old breed of pig was tall with long legs, short ears and a long intellectual-looking face. It was called the "greyhound pig" because of its slim appearance and long legs. It could jump over fences which were four feet in height. According to Phil it was impossible to fatten this type of pig but it was very easily trained and could respond to instructions given to it in Irish and in English. Furthermore, if this type of pig had the opportunity of living with a hedge schoolmaster it could also learn to respond to orders given to it in Latin!

A pig that was house-trained was referred to as an "educated" pig. Such a pig was allowed to wander around the smallholding during the day. It returned to the house at meal-times and took its proper place sitting in the circle around the cooking pot. The pig was placed beside the

"Don't forget—when you escape walk about a hundred yards
behind me."

youngest children. Sometimes the educated pig and the children squabbled over food.

Phil Purcel used to collect a herd of pigs, drive them to the boat and travel to England with them. The pigs with their slim bodies and long legs were very agile. Phil sold them to English farmers who thought they could make a profit on the deal by fattening the pigs with good food. Among the animals that Phil sold was one special pig that was particularly well educated. It was trained to jump fences and get away. Phil walked around the neighbour-hood whistling. His special pig was able to escape and walk about a hundred yards behind him. Once Phil was reunited with his special pig he would move on to the next town and sell it again! Anyone seeing Phil travelling from town to town simply saw a man walking by himself. It was unlikely that anyone would connect Phil with a pig wandering along the road some distance behind.

The Large White Ulster was another famous breed of local pig. It, as the name suggests, was very different from the slim, long-legged animal bred by Phil Purcel. It was a big pig that put weight on easily. This was an advantage because the heavier the pig the more money it raised when it was sold. Many Large White Ulster pigs became so overweight that folds of fat covered their eyes and they became blind.

Pigs were raised and slaughtered on farms until the 1930s when the Ulster Pig Marketing Scheme was introduced. This scheme forbade the slaughtering of pigs at home. They had to be killed in the abattoir. The Large White had a very thin skin so it was often damaged on the way there. Damaged pigs did not fetch as much money as undamaged ones so the Large White Ulster became less popular. The final blow to its production came with a change of fashion. The so-called "Wiltshire" cure became popular and replaced traditional methods of curing pigs. The Large White Ulster was unsuitable for that type of cure because it was too fat. The breed declined in numbers until it became extinct.

The coming of industry to nineteenth-century Belfast attracted workers who had been raised on farms to the city. They brought their old habits and farming skills with them. They often kept pigs and hens in the backyards of their terrace houses. Practically all the houses in areas like the Newtownards Road in Belfast had a pig and a few hens in the backyard.

A typical industrial hand would have lived in a street similar to Bloomfield Street off the Newtownards Road and worked in the shipyard belonging to Harland and Wolff. The keeping of pigs in backyards was common

Terraced house off Newtownards Road, Belfast

until the 1930s. Any man who kept a pig was called a "pig man." Pig men used to ask people in the surrounding area to keep left-over food and vegetable peelings for their pigs. Boys, known locally as "skins boys," walked along the back entries behind the terrace houses and collected each household's refuse to feed the area's pigs. This practice continued until the 1950s.

When I was a young child I lived with my parents in Orby Parade off the Castlereagh Road in Belfast. I remember my mother placing vegetable peelings, uneaten potatoes and other household refuse in a bucket that was kept in an outhouse. Each week a pig man, carrying a huge bucket, would open the outhouse door, remove my mother's bucket and empty its contents into his. The pig man, his trousers tucked into muddy wellington boots, looked rather incongruous as he went about his business in a surburban neighbourhood among the semi-detached houses.

Before legislation forbade it pigs were slaughtered at home. The animal was usually killed by being struck on the forehead with something heavy such as a sledge-hammer. Its throat was then cut and the carcase was hung up to bleed. After that boiling water was poured over the skin and it was scraped to remove hairs.

Nothing of the slaughtered pig was wasted. It provided bacon and ham, which were smoked for preservation. The liver, heart and trotters were also eaten. Pigs' intestines were used as sausage skins, blood was turned into black pudding and even the stomach was used, stuffed with bread and herbs, as a local version of haggis.

Meat on pigs' trotters was thought to be particularly tasty. There was a small butcher's shop at the bottom of the Albertbridge Road in Belfast. It was owned by Hugh

Gemmell, an amateur poet. He always had a verse pasted on his shop front advertising the excellence of the pigs' feet which he had for sale. Once, shortly after the Second World War, when the shop was being renovated, a corrugated, iron hoarding was placed in front of it. The following verse appeared on the hoarding:

> Behind this iron curtain,
> Gemmell's can't be seen
> But though his shop is hidden,
> His feet are still supreme.

Hens were very important to the farmer's wife because tradition decreed that she was allowed to keep any money she earned from them. This gave her a little independence. The value of forty hens was thought to be equal to that of one cow. Leghorns, Sussex and Irish bare-neck hens were breeds commonly found. The Irish bare-neck hen is particularly interesting. It has, as the name suggests, no feathers on its neck. When it perches in a tree, or a barn, it bears a passing resemblance to a vulture.

According to Ernest Scott, a local historian from Ballynure, horses were extremely important to farmers who had produce for sale. The only means of taking food to market before motorcars and lorries became common was to use a horse and cart. Ernest remembers helping his father load a cart before leaving home at three o'clock in the morning to travel to Belfast. They used to arrive in Belfast before seven o'clock and sell their goods at the market. They would have their breakfast in the Irish Temperance League café at the corner of May Street, near the City Hall. Breakfast consisted of an "Ulster Fry": bacon, egg, potato bread, soda bread and sometimes a

"Just think—I'm worth forty hens."

fried pancake as well. The café was warm and cosy and appeared particularly welcoming on a cold, wet morning in the middle of winter. According to Ernest the Temperance League organised cafés to keep men from drinking too much in public houses. Men had a tradition of going on the "tear." This meant that they disappeared into the local public house and stayed there for days—some say for weeks, or even months. Mothers, sweethearts and wives were expected to go on living normally until they returned. This practice of heavy drinking had a devastating effect on families.

Ernest remembers men ploughing with "half-Clydes-

dale" horses on his father's farm in Ballynure during the
1920s. (Half-Clydesdales had an Irish mare as mother and
a Clydesdale sire.) Most Irish farmers had horses smaller
than Clydesdales because they used them for pulling
traps and riding as well as providing power to work heavy
machinery and working in the fields. Sturdy crossbred
cobs with distinctive "skewbald," brown and white mark-
ings were common on small farms before the tractor was
invented. This type of horse is still popular with gypsies.

The characteristics of a good horse were described as
follows:

> Three traits of a bull: a bold walk, a strong
> neck and a hard forehead;
> Three traits of a fox: a light step, a look to the
> front and a glance to each side of the road;
> Three traits of a woman: a broad bosom, a
> slender waist and a short back;
> Three traits of a hare: a lively ear, a bright eye
> and a quick run against a hill.

According to folklore horses understand human speech.
They are capable of bringing luck. If a mare drops her
seventh foal in the open field, tradition suggests that the
field should be searched for a four-leafed shamrock. This
will keep its owner from being deceived by magicians.
Horses were thought to be able to see ghosts more easily
than humans and to be sensitive to places where evil has
occurred. They were thought to be unwilling to pass a
place where a murder has taken place.

Some people had the ability to calm horses. A man
called Sullivan, who lived near Newmarket, County Cork
around 1830 had a secret way of calming horses. He

would go into a stable with an unbroken horse, shut all doors and half an hour later lead out a horse notably calm and biddable. He travelled around the countryside calming horses for a guinea or two. He kept his method so secret that he did not even tell his son with the result that his skill died with him. The ability to calm horses was not confined to men. There was a woman who lived in County Kerry who possessed the skill.

Many famous horses have come from Ireland, such as Napoleon's famous white charger "Marengo." He was bred in County Wexford and bought by a Frenchman who presented him to the emperor at a later date. Strangely enough the charger ridden by Wellington at the battle of Waterloo also came from Ireland. It was bought at a fair at Cahirmee.

5

Markets, Fairs and Faking

The dates on which markets and fairs were held had great significance for most people in the past. Masters and servants, whether men, women or children, apprentices and journeymen, all had the right to leave their work for the day to meet their friends and enjoy the fun of the fair.

Markets and fairs meant serious business for many families as they tried to sell the animals and crops on which their livelihood depended. Towns which originally had a fair or a market are characterised by a wide main street or a large square where people could sell goods. Apart from farmers dealing in animals and produce and their wives selling butter, hens and eggs there were weavers selling linen and besom-sellers and rush dealers offering their wares. Rushes were tied into bundles and sold to flax-farmers who used them as ties for beets of flax. Ling, blue-blossomed heather, was pulled out by the roots on hilltops and trimmed to make the very useful brooms that were called besoms in Scotland and the north of Ireland.

There have been tremendous changes in transport and marketing during the past fifty years. New forms of entertainment have taken the crowds off the streets. These

At the Auld Lammas Fair, Balycastle, County Antrim

changes have led to the death of most fairs and markets. Some fairs, such as the famous Puck Fair at Killorglin in County Kerry, have survived the passage of time. So too have some weekly markets, such as those held in Dublin on Saturdays, in Newry on Thursdays and in Lisburn on Tuesdays.

The most ancient fairs are those of Lughnasa which celebrates the ancient god of the harvest. Through time the name Lughnasa changed to Lammas. Lammas fairs are held in August (Lughnasa is the Gaelic word for August). Their original purpose was to ensure fertility. Puck Fair at Killorglin and the Auld Lammas Fair at Ballycastle, County Antrim, are surviving examples of this type.

Puck Fair is unusual because each year a goat is chosen and crowned king. It is then put into a cage which is hung high above the fair while the people below drink, trade, enjoy street entertainments, have their fortunes told and generally have a good time. It is said that any young woman attending the fair will have a baby during the following year. My daughter was born during the spring of the year after I visited Puck Fair. I do not know if that is a coincidence or not!

The Auld Lammas Fair at Ballycastle is a rather more sober occasion. It does not have the benefit of a goat crowned as king. The tradition is much more prosaic: one simply buys a sticky, hard, honeycomb toffee called "yellow man" and dulse. Dulse is a type of seaweed collected from the shores around Ireland, dried and eaten. In the days when hunger stalked the land, dulse was a useful additional food during the long days of summer, when foodstores were running low and the next harvest was not ready. It is rich in vitamins and mineral salts including iodine. It has a salty taste and makes people thirsty, so that they are inclined to drink more than usual. As in Puck Fair, people go to Ballycastle to trade, have their fortunes told and enjoy the buskers and other forms of street entertainment.

Banbridge, County Down, like many other country towns, had a street market. The market was held on Mondays. Farm produce, flowers, linen, general goods and livestock were sold. It gradually lost popularity over the years until the last vestige left was a single street trader who sold plants on Mondays during the summer months. In addition to the weekly markets there were horse fairs. Most of the old fairs and markets died when a good transport system developed which enabled farmers to sell goods far afield. Some of the fairs were turned into sites for fun fairs.

There has been a recent attempt to revive some of the old fairs as tourist attractions. Hilltown has revived its Boley Fair and Dromore, County Down, again has an

The wide street in Banbridge is a sign that in the past a market was held in the town

annual horse fair. It is interesting to see horses led up the street showing their paces and watch people bargaining, although I have not seen anyone seal a bargain in the way my mother described. She told me that in her day the buyer and the seller spat on their own right hands. They then shook hands so that the spit on each hand was combined. It was traditional, once the bargain was sealed and money had exchanged hands, for the buyer to return a piece of silver to the seller as a "luck penny." Horses were an extremely important means of transport and remained so until the 1950s.

When I was a child, growing up in Belfast during that decade, pint bottles of milk were delivered to our house each day by a milkman, who had a cart and a horse called "Hamlet." The milkman told me he was expected to take Hamlet to the stables each night and attend to its needs. He was required to groom the horse, feed it and keep its stable-area clean. The milkman grieved when Hamlet was replaced by a van sometime towards the end of the '50s. Hamlet was replaced because it was much cheaper to buy petrol and maintain a van than it was to stable and look after a horse.

The milkman said his job became much more impersonal when his horse was replaced. Collecting a van was an entirely different thing to collecting Hamlet each morning because the horse always appeared pleased to see him. People would come out of their houses to talk to the horse; nobody paid any attention to the van! Hamlet had his own friends, people who regularly fed him tidbits such as lumps of sugar, bread or carrots. He remembered where there were treats to be had and often set off down the street on his own to his favourite houses. The milkman said Hamlet's behaviour added interest to his round. Our neighbours also missed Hamlet. They used to rush out quickly and pick up his droppings with a brush and shovel to put around their roses. The roses did not do so well once Hamlet had gone!

Horses played a considerable part in the life of Belfast. The city once had horse-drawn trams as public transport. Milk, coal and bread were delivered to householders by horse and cart. Each city bakery, and there were many, would have needed about a hundred horses in its stables to make sure that its product was distributed efficiently.

Horses were essential to farmers with sufficient land to produce a surplus. They were needed to prepare the land for growing crops, to help with the harvest and to take the produce to market. Dealers hired gangs of men to bring horses to fairs. Each man rode on the bare back of one horse and led about six others, strung together by their halters. The men were usually rough and poorly clad but affable and jolly. They stayed with their charges and often slept beside them out on the streets. Horses and donkeys would begin to arrive for a horse fair several days before the event. By the time the big day arrived the town concerned would be very congested. People living in terrace houses along streets holding fairs had to go in and out through the back doors because their front doors were often blocked by livestock.

The Irish have a reputation for kindliness. Local inhabitants were often very good to the men tending animals. Robert Grange, who lived as a boy in Mill Lane, Ballyclare, remembers how his mother used to take refreshments, such as a bowl of broth, a cup of tea or a farl of soda bread to the horse handler outside her door.

During the fair dealers would invite seemingly nonchalant buyers who were strolling up and down to try out the stock. The animals would be standing shoulder to shoulder in a line along the footpath. One would be chosen and raced up and down the road to show its shape and prowess. This practice, which is still common in horse fairs held today, is a trial of wind and limb. It also shows how an animal places its feet when it walks. This is crucial if the horse is intended for use in potato or turnip drills. A splay-footed horse would make a mess of any drill.

Running horses among people can be dangerous. Sometimes spectators were killed. The *Belfast News Letter* for Wednesday 21 May 1879 describes how a man was killed when a horse kicked back and struck him on the upper portion of his body.

Charlie McCourt, an old age pensioner who lives in Banbridge, told me how as a boy he watched men faking horses, that is making old sick horses look young and lively, in an entry off Dromore Street at "the foot of the town." The horses were sold later in the day at the market in the town. According to Charlie sickly animals were doctored to look "wonderful." Old horses had their grey hairs dyed with Indian ink or touched up with boot polish to make them look younger.

It is possible to tell a horse's age from its teeth so some horses had their mouths doctored. The teeth at the back of the mouth were removed to make it look younger. Other teeth were filed down and a fake black spot placed in the middle of each one also to give a younger appearance. If a horse's face was pathetic-looking, with sunken eyes, then the hollows were injected with water. This gave the face a nice rounded appearance. Horses with broken wind were fed normal food mixed with lead shot to disguise the defect.

Lame horses were inspected very carefully. It required great expertise to make a lame horse appear normal. There were two methods of doing it. One was to remove the shoe from the good leg, the other was to kick the good leg hard. Both methods caused the animal to walk evenly. It depended on the individual horse which was the better method to use!

Bad-tempered horses were injected with dope to quieten them down so that they appeared gentle at sale time. The effect lasted a few days, after which the horse reverted to type. Another trick to quieten a bad-tempered horse was to tie a wad of tobacco around its bit. The horse would appear quiet as it contentedly chewed!

Skewbald horses, that is, horses with coats of two colours, were thought to be unlucky. They were often dyed so that they appeared to be one colour. There are many tales of people who bought a horse at a fair and rode it through the rain. By the time they reached home the dye had washed off the animal and it looked very different from when it had been bought.

Charlie also told me that an animal could be made to look a lot livelier by sticking a wad of tobacco up its backside. Apparently this cruel treatment made it hold its tail out with spirit and move faster. He said he remembered one poor old horse in particular. It came in with its head hanging down and its tail between its legs. It looked as if it could hardly place one foot past the other. After the tobacco treatment it was revived as if by magic and shot out of the yard like greased lightning with its tail well up! Ginger was another substance used stuck up an animal's backside to make it appear livelier. Charlie said that all animals could be given the tobacco or ginger treatment to make them appear livelier. He saw cows, sheep and pigs as well as horses being treated in this manner.

There is a tale told of a man from Ballymena who had a very lethargic sow for sale. The animal was so slow it could hardly move. He took it to the market in the town, gave it the ginger treatment and sat beside it all day trying to sell it. He could find nobody foolish enough to buy the animal so, very depressed, he set off home. The animal staggered along in front of him, very, very slowly. Filled with impatience he tried kicking it to make it go a bit

"Never mind what the horse feels like—I'll make it look better."

"Mummy, Mummy, come quickly! Dobbin's rump has changed colour since we bought him yesterday."

faster. The pig did not respond so he shoved some ginger up its backside. This time the ginger had a more marked effect. The animal ran so fast he could not keep up with it so in desperation he gave himself the ginger treatment too!

Pork was sold in open markets until slaughter in abattoirs became common. Farmers carried their pork in carts and lined up outside the market house to have the carcases weighed. A farmer who did not receive a good price for his pork was in a very awkward position. Meat decayed quickly in the days before refrigeration became available. It was difficult for even a large family to dispose of a whole pig before it decayed.

A good market had a public weighbridge and a reliable operator. The commissioners appointed to inquire into the state of fairs and markets in Ireland in 1853 uncovered a lot of dishonesty. Many of the weighbridges had two sets of weights, one for buying and one for selling. Other weighbridges had slides which allowed a bar of lead to be inserted so that a true weight was not obtained. Farmers selling live animals, such as pigs, cows, sheep and horses, were free to take their animals home again if they were not offered a reasonable price. They could always try again at a later fair.

Fowl dealers visited markets regularly to buy birds for resale. Some dealers travelled around the countryside bargaining for birds at farmhouses. They often travelled on bicycles with up to eight half-dead fowl tied to the handlebars. Fowl were usually sold to dealers in bundles of five or six. Most bundles contained a dud or weakling along with good birds.

In the past hygiene was sadly lacking at markets and fairs—indeed it was lacking in shops as well. I remember an old shop on the Castlereagh Road in Belfast. It sold hardware and "country" butter. The butter had a delicious flavour and so was much in demand. The shop and the old man who owned it were absolutely filthy, covered in grime. The place was extremely untidy; yet if one went in and asked for something small, say a pot mender, the owner would grunt, come out from behind the counter and begin fiddling among the untidy, dust-covered pile of goods which littered the shop floor. He invariably managed to find whatever was required within seconds. Believe it or not, the country butter was concealed within the pile. It was produced with a flourish, banged upon the counter, unwrapped, the required amount cut from the slab, banged into shape by the man's dirty hands and wrapped in greaseproof paper. The butter was smuggled into Belfast from country areas and sold on the "black market" during and for some time after the Second World War when butter was rationed. My mother was a regular customer. She used to take the butter home, cut a thin slice off the outer edges and feed it to the cat. She thought the inside of the butter, not touched by the shopkeeper's hands, was clean enough. She said dirty butter had a bad taste.

My grandmother showed me how to test butter. She said that a lot of the butter sold was rancid or oversalted so that it tasted awful. Housewives used to travel around the market-stalls and ask to taste the butter. The stall owners would unwrap the butter exposing the upper surface. The housewife used the nail of her forefinger to scrape a little butter off the sample. If she liked the taste she asked for an amount, say a pound, to be cut off the slab. If she did not like the taste of the butter she refused to buy it. Granny said she found it necessary to watch stall owners and make sure she obtained butter from the slab she had tasted and not from another slab in at the back of the stall. She had been very upset when, as a new bride, she had gone to buy butter at Belfast Market and been duped. She tasted the butter and it was good. The stall holder turned around very quickly holding the piece in her hands, as if she had been distracted by something, shouted across to another stall holder behind her, turned around again with butter still held in her hands and cut the required amount off. When granny took the butter home she discovered that it was ghastly and had to throw it out. She realised the stall holder had changed slabs when she turned round.

Hiring fairs were held on 1 May and 1 November. The first day of the hiring fair was traditionally a holiday so there was a great air of festivity. Young men and women

Market Day

packed some food with their belongings, which they made into a parcel to tuck under their arms, and set off to enjoy themselves. However, their going to the fair had a serious purpose. Before it ended they had to make sure of being hired for the coming six months. The men and women seeking employment stood in traditional places, men along one side of the street, women along the other, and waited for potential employers to come and talk to them. They held their belongings proudly under their arms as a status symbol. It was important for the parcel to be large as that suggested prudence and comparative wealth due to the ability to earn a high wage. These parcels were often packed with straw to make them appear larger. Being interviewed at a hiring fair could be a humiliating experience. Potential employers were at liberty to ask very personal questions and to attempt to find out how strong individuals were by feeling their muscles.

I once met an old man in a doctor's surgery in Banbridge who said that fighting in the Second World War had been a horrendous experience. Nevertheless, he felt it had an overall helpful effect on his life. Before the war he had worked as a farm labourer, hiring himself out each May and November. He said there were good, generous hirers who provided good homes for their labourers. Unfortunately they were difficult to find. If a worker found a good billet he or she was very careful not to give offence and made sure that work was done in a pleasant, efficient way. As a result the majority of jobs were unofficially filled before the hiring fair. People in this happy situation simply went to the fair and struck up another agreement with their old bosses within the first five minutes. They then had the rest of the day off. As my man reported there was at the time a high level of unemployment so he, along with others in the same position, had to hang around, feeling humiliated and receiving unreasonable offers from miserly individuals. He escaped the system by signing up when the war started. He learnt a trade in the army and came back after the war as a skilled labourer who never again had difficulty in obtaining employment.

The individual who had been hired was given a small amount of money, usually a silver shilling, to seal the deal. He or she was then entitled to a small wage and "free" board and lodging until the next hiring fair. The wage, minus the shilling, became due at the end of the period in question. If the hired individual became disgruntled and left employment before the time was finished the contract was said to be null and void and no money was paid. Many dishonest farmers tried to make life impossible for their hired hands towards the end of the period in the hope that they would leave hiring and be unable to obtain their wages. Some hired hands were treated as members of the family, others were very badly treated, expected to sleep in the barn, have their frugal meals placed on the doorstep and eat alone outside.

It is a way of life that has gone and it would be sentimental to mourn its passing. Much of the filth and cruelty that used to be associated with handling animals has disappeared and the noise and drunkenness that accompanied fairs is a thing of the past.

6

The Great Hunger

The Antrim coast road stretches from Larne to Cushendall. It is a beautiful road with spectacular headlands and wonderful views, and it passes through picturesque villages and towns. Yet like many other places in Ireland, this was the scene of appalling tragedy. People starved to death here. There is a memorial carved into the limestone on the landward side of the road, about a quarter of a mile north-west of Garron Point, near Carnlough. It is known as the "Famine Stone."

Frances Anne Vane
Marchioness of Londonderry
Being Connected with This Province
By the Double Ties of Birth and Marriage
And Being Desirous To Hand Down To Posterity
An Imperishable Memorial to Ireland's Affliction
And England's Generosity
In the Year 1846-47
Unparalleled in the Annals of Human Suffering
Hath Engraved This Stone

Fair tablet fashioned by the Almighty's Hand
To guard these confines of the sea and land
No longer shalt thou meet the stranger's sight,
A polished surface of unmeaning white,
But bid him ponder on the days of yore,
When plague and famine stalked along the shore,
And pale Irene veiled her drooping head,
Like Rachel weeping for her children dead,
Tell him to assuage these pangs and fears
Britannia gave her bounty with her tears
And hear this record, though in phrases crude,
Of England's love and Ireland's gratitude.

There are two lines written in Irish underneath the above inscription meaning, "O give thanks unto the Lord for He is good; who remembered us in our low estate, for His mercy endureth forever." Psalm CXXXVI: 1, 23 iii October MDCCCXLIX"

People with nationalistic sympathies destroyed the lines written in Irish and part of the text during the 1920s. Some time afterwards a bronze plaque was placed beside the original text. The plaque contains a transcription of the original message.

What happened? Why is there reference to plague and famine?

Local folklore suggests that the road was built during a terrible famine in 1833. The road was supposed to provide a means for starving people to earn food, and payment for a day's work was a small bowl of rice. It is said that forty people, men, women and children, died for each mile of the road constructed.

How did such a tragedy happen?

There were many famines in Ireland and one

Red Bay, Antrim Coast Road

devastating one (1846-47) which became known as the "great hunger." The history of the famines is very complicated. Not all areas were affected equally. Famines in nineteenth-century Ireland were caused by failure of potato crops. Potatoes formed the staple diet of people in poorer areas. Meat was rarely eaten except at Easter or Christmas. Poor families could not afford to eat meat and even those who reared a pig were forced to sell it to pay the rent.

Potatoes, with the addition of milk or buttermilk, form a balanced diet. The very poor who did not even have sufficient potatoes to eat used to undercook what little they had because hard, underdone potatoes are more difficult to digest than soft ones. They stay in the stomach for a longer time and cut down the number of hunger pains felt.

The potato crops failed because of disease, usually potato blight fungus, *Phytophthora infestans*. Spores of the fungus landed on the potato leaves, grew down through a leaf pore and rapidly killed the plant. If rain washed the fungus off the leaves it entered the ground and attacked potato tubers turning them rotten.

During the eighteenth and early nineteenth centuries Ireland's population grew rapidly. Most people lived at subsistence level. They found day-to-day existence difficult and had no resources to help them survive a misfortune. The 1842 census tells us that nearly half of the rural population lived in sod houses. Those evicted for non-payment of rent and others who were unable to get work dug holes in banks and lived in them or tried to devise shelters in bog holes. Some lived in ditches with roofs made of branches to cover them.

People were so poor that furniture was a luxury. In 1837 the parish of Tullahobagly in County Donegal had

Cave, Red Bay, Antrim Coast Road, once a human habitation

a population of 9000. These people owned among them 10 beds, 95 chairs and 243 stools. Many people fell into debt. Middlemen who collected debt were called "gombeen men." I remember being very naughty as a small child and my grandmother saying to me, "You'd better be a good girl or the gombeen man will get you." I had no idea what a gombeen man was but the menace reflected in my grandmother's voice sounded terrifying and I behaved. People falling into arrears with their debt were evicted. Eviction removed them from their homes and their livelihood. They were left to starve to death because there was no state benefit. Evicted people had nowhere to go but the workhouse. According to my grandmother, that was a fate worse than death.

The Irish are fond of children. In the days before old age pensions children acted as insurance against destitution

The former workhouse at Dunfanaghy, County Donegal

in old age. Children were expected to look after their parents, to run the farm and do their best to ensure that aged parents did not suffer want. Large families were normal. The demand for land increased as the population grew. Farms which had been divided by middlemen and landlords were divided again by the people themselves. Parents allowed their children to have a portion of their land because the alternative was to turn them out to starve. These children in their turn allowed their children to use their land. In a comparatively short time many families were settled on land that could provide food reasonably for only one. Competition for land caused the rents to become enormously high, 80 to a 100 per cent higher than in England.

In the mid-nineteenth century there had been no scientific breeding of potatoes or research into crop failure and as a result most potato crops were prone to disease. There had been many failures over the years. In 1821 and 1822 the potato crop failed in Munster and Connacht while in 1832, 1833, 1834 and 1836 a large number of districts had poor potato crops because of the diseases known as potato dry-rot and potato leaf-curl.

In 1845 the potato crop looked as if it was going to be particularly good. On 25 July in that year *The Times* reported that an early harvest was expected. When the potatoes came to be gathered they appeared good but they turned into a stinking mass within days. This was serious but it did not affect the whole country. Real disaster struck in 1846. Captain Mann, a coastguard worker, wrote, "I shall never forget the change in one week in August. On the first occasion I had passed over thirty-two miles thickly studded with potato fields in full bloom. The next time the face of the whole country was changed, the stalk remained bright green but the leaves were all scorched black. It was the work of a night." In 1846 the harvest was generally bad and poor people were at the end of their resources. Autumn turned into winter. Blackberries, nettles, rosehips, chickweed, hazelnuts and all other forms of free food disappeared.

Horror stories were reported. A woman and her two children were found dead on their farm at Caheragh, County Cork. Their bodies were half eaten by dogs. Nicholas Cummins, a Cork magistrate, visited Skibbereen in December 1846. He was surprised to find the place apparently empty. He entered the first hovel to see what was happening and found six famished, ghastly skeleton-like figures lying on filthy straw. At first he thought they were dead but low moaning showed them to be alive, a man, a woman and four children. They had fever. Within minutes he was surrounded by 200 skeletal people. Later in the day he saw a mother, herself suffering from fever, drag the body of her young daughter out of her home and leave it half covered with stones. In another house he found seven wretched people, so weak they could not move, lying huddled under a cloak. One was dead but the others could not move themselves, never mind move a corpse.

The climate in Ireland is usually mild. Normally there is very little snow and semi-tropical plants flourish in the gardens of the south and west. The winter of 1846-47 was "the most severe in living memory" and the longest. It seemed as if nature had joined Ireland's enemies. Snow fell early in November and was followed by continuous frost and icy gales. Relief schemes were organised but they proved very inefficient. On 24 October Denis McKennedy died while working on Road No 1, in the western division of West Carbery, County Cork. He had not been paid since 10 October. Dr Daniel Donovan and Dr Patrick Due carried out a post-mortem. They found that the dead man had died from starvation. There was no food in his stomach or in his small intestine. The large intestine was found to contain a "portion of undigested raw cabbage mixed with excrement." The inquest found that he had "died of starvation caused by gross neglect of the Board of Works."

Food, such as grain, was actually exported from Ireland during the famine. The government, with its belief in free enterprise, felt that food exported from Ireland could be sold at high prices and the money used to import cheap food for sale.This did not work because large numbers of people never bought food. They simply grew potatoes and ate them. The more humane landlords organised soup-kitchens to help their hungry tenants. Eventually the government developed the idea and organised soup for the starving.

Good soup with a meal cake, or a piece of bread, is of sound nutritional value and generous people, often with only modest means, kept hundreds of people alive by distributing it. However, a lot of the soup was terrible. The Rt Hon James Grattan of Vicarstown, Queen's County had thirty gallons of soup distributed. It was made from one oxhead, without the tongue, twenty-eight pounds of turnips, three and a half pounds of onions, seven pounds of carrots, twenty-one pounds of pea meal, fourteen pounds of Indian corn meal and water. The local school-master described it as a "vile compound" and the people, after one trial meal, refused to eat it because it gave them "bowel complaints."

There was no legal register of deaths during the period so the number of people who died is unknown. More people died of "famine fever" than of starvation. Bodies weakened by malnutrition are more prone to disease than healthy ones so people caught common diseases, such as dysentery, diphtheria, scarlet fever, tuberculosis, influenza and so on and died from them. Typhus and relapsing fevers were also present. Both these fevers are carried by lice and both were already familiar in Ireland.

Typhus is caused by microscopic, rod-shaped organisms entering the blood. The louse catches the organism by feeding on infected blood. The organisms multiply inside the louse and pass out with its droppings. They are very infectious. If louse droppings come in contact with the slightest cut on human skin the organisms can enter and cause disease. If an individual slaps a louse and kills it the organisms are released and touching the dead louse is dangerous. Dried louse droppings form a fine infectious dust that can enter the body through the eyes, or even be inhaled. This meant that many people, who had never been near a louse and who helped the famine victims, caught typhus and died.

Typhus is a terrible disease. The infecting organisms attack the small blood vessels of the body, especially those of the brain and the skin. The patient becomes unrecognisable as the face swells and turns dark in colour. In Ireland the dark-coloured face has given typhus the common name of black fever. The patient becomes delirious, the temperature rises and the body begins to feel as if it is burning so the patient becomes liable to jump out of the window or into a river in an attempt to cool down. Then a rash appears. The patient feels awful pain, vomits and develops ghastly sores that can turn into gangrene so that fingers and sometimes toes are lost. Another symptom of typhus is the terrible smell. William

Bennett, a member of the Society of Friends, described it as "an almost intolerable stench." Dr Crumpe, medical officer of Tralee gaol, said that when he opened the door to visit a typhus patient he was "forcibly driven back by the smell" and he was always "seized with the most violent retching."

Relapsing fever was another type of disease common during the famine. It is also caused by a louse which has swallowed infected blood. The infecting organisms do not pass out with louse excrement but are released if the louse is slightly damaged. They enter human blood through the skin. Within a few hours of being infected the patient runs a high temperature and begins vomiting. The vomiting continues for several days and then a crisis occurs with a lot of sweating. This is followed by absolute exhaustion. Six or seven days later the patient relapses and has another crisis. If the patient manages to survive three or four relapses recovery is possible. Relapsing fever is often accompanied by jaundice so that the patient's skin turns yellow. This gave relapsing fever the common name of yellow fever.

Cholera caused many deaths in Ireland during an epidemic in 1831 and 1832. The disease reappeared in Europe in 1848 and advanced towards Ireland. The first case was reported in Belfast Lunatic Asylum in November 1848. It became epidemic throughout the city and spread to the rest of Ireland during 1849. In Belfast cholera victims were buried in a mound in Friar's Bush graveyard, which is beside the Ulster Museum on the Stranmillis Road.

Cholera is caused by a bacteria which contaminates food and water. During epidemics the death rate may be as high as 50 per cent. Epidemic cholera is usually in the form of *cholera gravis*. There are three stages. During the first stage of the illness the patient suddenly becomes very ill, suffering from vomiting and diarrhoea. The limbs become very sore and then violent cramps are felt in the abdomen. The patient is restless, thirsty and feels exhausted. The eyeballs become sunken and the voice husky. This stage lasts about twelve hours.

During the second stage the patient undergoes a collapse. The surface of the body becomes colder and colder, the skin turns purple in colour and the voice is reduced to a whisper, and the patient may die. In epidemic cases this stage lasts between one and two hours. The temperature of the body may rise after death. Cholera has another strange effect after death. It can cause muscular contractions so that the victim's limbs move. If the patient survives the second stage of cholera the third stage is reached during which there is a gradual improvement. The temperature comes down and the pulse returns to normal. People began to whitewash houses at this time because the lime in the whitewash destroyed disease-causing germs.

Before the potato famine people believed that to be forced to leave Ireland was the most awful thing that could happen to them. Transportation was the most dreaded of sentences for criminals. Now starving, desperate people began leaving a country that appeared cursed. Tens of thousands fled across the sea. Unfortunately they brought disease with them.

As Ireland became depopulated the pressure for space decreased. There was no need to cultivate hilltop ground. To this day the outline of lazy-beds, once used for growing potatoes, may be traced beneath the heather on hilltops such as Belfast's Cave Hill, Slieve Gullion in County

Armagh, the Glens of Antrim, and on hilly ground throughout the country.

My great-grandmother's maiden name was Martha Cooper. She died in Belfast in 1942 aged 84 years. She was the granddaughter of Sammy Cooper, a nailer, who lived with his family in a house with a small garden, in Antrim. She told my grandmother that *her* mother remembered the famine vividly. I do not know if she was referring to the great famine (1846-47) or to another period of famine. Apparently, one of Sammy Cooper's jobs was to ring the church bell each day so that the "poor people" would know to come for their soup. Sometimes his wife rang the bell for him. He told her not to go near the "poor people" because it could be dangerous. She could become diseased. She used to watch from a distance as ill-clad, starving wretches came and queued for food. She wished she could help. She said if she had been starving she would have pushed her way to the front of the queue. These people stood quietly in depressed lines.

A friend told me of the "famine" memories in his family. His ancestors lived near Coleraine, County Derry and were so poor they did not have plates. They cooked potatoes in their one pot, drained them and held them in their hands as they ate. During the famine they were given Indian corn. They used the corn to make a gruel, dug four holes in their earthen floor (one for each member of the family), poured the gruel into the holes and survived by eating like dogs.

Today, nearly one hundred and fifty years later, whenever I remember the sadness expressed by my grandmother when she talked about the famine, I feel rage that so many people starved to death. What could have been done to avert the disaster? What is being done for starving people today in such places as Ethiopia? Are the developed nations, with the advantages provided by means of transport and modern medical knowledge, any more successful in preventing people from starving to death than those who too late attempted to help the Irish in the past?

7

Emigration

Emigration did not come easily to the Irish as they loved their homeland. This love has survived through generations of emigrant families. It is impossible for any Irish person to visit the USA, Canada, the British mainland, Australia or New Zealand without being told by numerous people, "My family originally came from Ireland." During the early eighteenth century there was comparatively little emigration. Whatever little there was originated in Ulster, mainly of Presbyterians of Scottish descent who wanted to better their lot. They were not paupers. They took money and experience with them.

The emigration caused by the great famine was of unskilled people into more skilled communities. The Irish poor had nothing to bring with them. They lived in the poorest of conditions in their new homes and were despised by other residents. Very few people who fled the famine became prosperous. It was not until the second and third generations that native Irish intelligence began to assert itself and the children and grandchildren of the poor famine emigrants became rich and powerful in their new lands.

The nineteenth-century timber trade from British North

Replica of Belfast docks and emigrant ship, Ulster Museum Folk Park, Omagh, Co Tyrone

America provided a way of escape. Ships came over loaded with timber. There was no demand for European goods in the New World so the ships had either to sail back carrying nothing but ballast or take passengers. Wooden berths were put up between decks and in the early days passengers had to bring their own food. The shipowners supplied fuel and water. Fares might seem low but the average family had to save for about one year in order to raise the money. It was possible to travel to Quebec for two or three pounds.

By 1845 the transportation of emigrants had reached the stage where larger profits were being made by the passenger trade than the timber trade. This was encouraged by the British government because it allowed the timber to be sold at a low price.

As the winter of the famine 1846-47 dragged on life became so terrible that people grew more and more desperate to leave. Emigrant ships faced the Atlantic in winter for the first time in history. Most Irish emigrants wanted to go to the United States. They went by a roundabout route. American ships were safer and better than British ones but they were more expensive. In 1842 the fare from Belfast to Quebec on a British ship was six pounds for a man, his wife and four children. The fare to New York for the same family was twenty-one pounds. Most emigrants sailed to Quebec then crossed the border into the States. They settled primarily around the north-eastern cities of Boston, New York, Pittsburgh and Philadelphia.

The Irish were so anxious to escape from their benighted land that they were content to suffer great hardship during the voyage. They felt that they had nothing to lose, apart from their lives and those lives were in danger at home. Their desperation led to the existence of the "coffin" ships. These were very old, overcrowded hulks, often short of legal quotas of food and water. They began to leave from smaller and smaller ports such as Ballina, Westport, Tralee and Killala.

The *Elizabeth and Sarah* was a typical example of a coffin ship. It sailed from Killala, County Mayo in July 1846 and arrived in Quebec in September. The captain was so incompetent that the passage took eight weeks, about twice as long as the normal duration of the voyage. The passenger list showed 212 names but the ship carried 276 people. She should have had 12,532 gallons of water, but had only 8700 gallons stored in leaking casks. The Passenger Act of 1842 ordered that 7lbs of provisions be given out each week to each passenger. No food was ever given out on the *Elizabeth and Sarah*. The ship had thirty-six berths, four of which were taken by the crew. The 276 passengers shared the remaining thirty-two berths, or slept on the floor. There was no toilet of any kind on board so conditions within the vessel became disgusting. Passengers were starving and tortured by thirst. Forty-two of them died in the course of the voyage.

A coffin ship sailing from Westport is said to have sunk within sight of land, watched by relatives and other loved ones, to whom the emigrants had just said goodbye. There was not a single survivor. Ships leaving from large ports such as Dublin, Belfast, Sligo and Waterford were comparatively well equipped.

Officials in Canada were worried about the effect of the disease-ridden Irish on their country. They decided that all ships carrying passengers up the St Lawrence should stop at a quarantine station on Grosse Isle, thirty miles down the river. Vessels with sickness on board were to be detained and the sick taken off for treatment in the quarantine hospital. The medical officer in charge of the quarantine station, Dr Douglas, asked on 19 February 1847 for $3000 to make preparation for the expected springtime immigration. He was given less than $300 and allowed a small steamer to ply between Grosse Isle and Quebec. He was also given permission to hire a sailing vessel, provided he could do so for $50 for the season.

During April the hospital became overcrowded so Dr. Douglas asked for permission to build a new shed for $150. He was granted $135. By 24 May all accommodation was dangerously overcrowded. There were 695 people in hospital and 164 on board ship waiting to land. On 26 May thirty vessels with 10,000 emigrants on board were waiting at Grosse Isle. By 31 May forty vessels were waiting in a line extending two miles down the St Lawrence. There were 1,100 cases of fever on Grosse Isle, the patients being tended in tents, sheds or laid out in rows in the little church. There was an equal number on board the ships waiting to be taken off. At least another 45,000 emigrants were expected.

The emigrants were in a terrible state when they landed. They tottered off the ships—feeble, spectre-like wretches who died in their thousands. They died and the doctors and nurses who tended them died. Equipment in the hospitals was practically non-existent. Bedding had been sent down but there was nothing to put it on and it soon became soaked on the ground. Medical staff became unobtainable.

Over 100,000 emigrants left Ireland for British North America in 1847. It has been estimated that 20,000 died in Canada and at least 25,000 people had been treated in Canadian hospitals while 17,000 died at sea. One of the commissioners for emigration in the United States wrote, "If crosses and tombs could be erected on the water the whole route of the emigration vessels from Europe to America would have long since assumed the appearance of a cemetery."

Most emigrants worked very hard in their new homes and attempted to save money to send back to loved ones left behind in Ireland. This gave rise to the saying "money from America," meaning a windfall.

8

Banshees, Leprechauns, Fairies and Giants

In the past people tended to be very superstitious because, without the benefit of modern scientific knowledge, they lacked understanding of the causes of such things as disease, changes in the weather, organic decay and the like. Events that could not be explained were thought to be due to supernatural beings such as fairies. Irish folklore contains many references to different types of fairy. They were referred to as "the wee folk" or "the good people" but it was held that only those who believed in their existence were ever likely to see them.

According to tradition there once was a great war in heaven between God and the devil. The fairies took no part in the fight. They remained neutral throughout. The war ended when God managed to throw the devil into hell. God said to the fairies, "You cannot stay in heaven because you did not join with me in the fight against the devil, on the other hand it would be wrong for you to go to hell as you did not fight against me." He cast the fairies out of heaven and some of them landed on the earth, others landed under the earth and some ended up in the sea. It was because it was believed that they originally came from heaven that fairies are thought to be immortal.

Elizabeth Andrews in her book *Ulster Folk Lore* suggests that a primitive, pigmy race once existed in Ireland and that this race lived in underground chambers called souterrains. That would explain why ordinary people claimed to have heard music coming from under the ground. An individual catching sight of a member of the pigmy race would believe that a fairy had been sighted.

There is a genetic disease called achondroplastic dwarfism that is passed from one generation to the next. An achondroplastic dwarf is a perfectly normal individual who has shorter arms and legs than usual. The defect is obvious at birth. The dwarf will not grow any larger than the average six- or seven-year-old child. In the past people had a very unsympathetic attitude to pain, suffering and misfortune. They believed these things were caused by wicked behaviour. As a result defective children were concealed because they gave rise to gossip. Friends and neighbours would wonder what sin the family had committed to deserve such a punishment. Even Queen Victoria was not immune. She kept her backward son hidden. At least some families with achondroplastic dwarf children would have kept them hidden. Perhaps an individual catching a glimpse of an achondroplastic dwarf would have believed that a fairy had been sighted. The dwarf's family would have had no wish to shatter the illusion.

My grandmother, Elizabeth Henry, died on 17 March 1951, aged 71 years. She was born in 1879. She had a very great friend called Maud Browne. Maud was an achondroplastic dwarf who had been brought up in an orphanage. She did not know anything about her parents. Apparently she had been found as a newborn baby beside a rath, one of many prehistoric structures that are to be found throughout Ireland that people regarded as the home of the fairies. Maud said that she was told that she had been left out for the fairies to claim as their own but she was not a fairy, just a perfectly normal being, trapped inside an odd-looking body. If she had been hidden rather than abandoned she might have been mistaken for a fairy.

It was thought unlucky to build a house on the site of a rath or on the side of a fairy hill. (There is one of these hills near Cushendall as the local people will tell you.) Nobody should interfere with a fairy thorn—that solitary tree which is often to be found in the middle of a field. There are many tales around the countryside of people interfering with fairy thorns and suffering misfortune as a consequence. One of the most interesting is about the British Enkalon factory at Antrim. Apparently there was a fairy thorn on the site. It held up development of the

The Fairy Mountain, Tieverragh, Cushendall, County Antrim

factory as it was impossible to find anybody who would uproot it. Eventually a man came forward who said he did not believe in fairies and all that nonsense. He removed the thorn with a bulldozer. Later in the day the bulldozer fell into a hole in the ground in the field that had held the fairy thorn and the man was injured.

Banshees are the most misunderstood fairies in Ireland. They are softhearted, harmless creatures yet their appearance gives rise to the most profound fear. Banshees are female, with an awesome appearance. They are usually very beautiful with pale faces and long, flowing, dark hair. Only the old families of Ireland have banshees associated with them. The spirit appears to warn of imminent danger of death. If a person is about to die it is useful to know it so that affairs may be put into order, old grievances settled and finals accounts rendered. The banshee does not cause death, simply warns that it is likely. Banshees are softhearted. They are very upset at the idea of a death. That is why they sit and cry whenever they make their appearance. If a crowd of banshees appears and starts singing and clapping their hands that means someone very important is about to die.

An old lady whose family name was Cassidy and who lived in a house near Melmore Head in County Donegal claimed that she saw crowds of banshees wailing for six nights before the First World War was declared and that the same thing happened before the declaration of the Second World War.

The current president of Ards Historical Association, a retired doctor, told me that about fifty years ago he visited a patient, who was a retired schoolmistress. She lived on the Ards peninsula and when he called she was very upset. The previous day she had received a letter from her brother, who lived in America, saying he intended to come home to Ireland on a visit. That night the "family's little lady" appeared on the wall outside her bedroom window, weeping and wailing throughout the night. The doctor was still with his patient when a boy appeared with a telegram from the States. It told her that her brother had had a very serious heart attack and was not expected to live. However, the brother *did* recover and was able to visit his sister at a later date. The doctor, who came from County Tyrone, told me that when he was a boy he was acquainted with a family who had a daughter who had emigrated to America. One night the family banshee appeared to her and not unexpectedly she became very upset. She wired home to ask if anything was wrong and received a wire saying that her father had died on the day the banshee appeared.

According to tradition there is a banshee associated with the O'Neill family of Shane's Castle near Antrim. There is a sculpted face in the wall of the castle which has the features of the family banshee. When the banshee appears with her warning, the features of the stone face become more pronounced.

Leprechauns are another type of fairy. They are shoemakers and dress in green with large, black hats with a buckle at the front. In times of trouble they watch where people hide their gold so they know where to find it. There is always gold at the end of a rainbow! Fairies must always obey humans so anyone lucky enough to catch a leprechaun may demand a crock of gold. Leprechauns do not like parting with their treasure and are very cunning. They usually manage to trick the human into letting them go free, leaving their stores of gold intact.

O'Hare's Bar in Carlingford, County Louth, has a suit

of leprechaun clothes and some bones displayed in a case. The late publican, PJ O'Hare, said they were brought in by a man who found them in the mountains behind the village. Many people appear to take this very seriously. The tourist board organises leprechaun hunts each spring. A crock of gold is hidden in the mountains and licences are sold enabling individuals to search for the gold and keep anything found.

The cluricaun is an odd sort of fairy. It, like the leprechaun, is solitary and dresses with unfairylike homeliness. Cluricauns are very rare, especially in the north of Ireland. They spend their time drinking and becoming drunk in gentlemen's cellars. Some people argue that cluricauns do not exist as a separate entity. They believe cluricauns are simply leprechauns with bad habits.

The *Fear Dearg,* or Red Man, is also like a leprechaun. He wears a red coat and a red hat and spends his life

O'Hare's Bar, Carlingford, County Louth

playing practical jokes. Unfortunately Red Men possess a rather macabre sense of humour so their practical jokes are usually gruesome and nasty.

Fairy mistresses called leanhaun shee are also thought to exist. The leanhaun shee are very beautiful. They fall in love with mortal men and tempt them to make love. If the man consents, he becomes enslaved and cannot escape, unless he finds another victim to replace him in his mistress's affections. If he cannot he is doomed. He will sicken and die. He cannot obtain peace. In the afterlife he is condemned to wander the earth for ever as a ghost. On the other hand, if he manages to resist the charms of the leanhaun shee she becomes enslaved to him. Leanhaun shees often inspire their victims to write great poetry. Tradition suggests that is why many of the poets in Ireland died young.

Case containing leprechaun suit and bones

The ordinary fairies are dainty individuals with wings. They, like the other types, are thought to live in fairy forts or raths and to leave changelings in place of humans. In the past the nature of disease was not understood. The onset of serious disease may change the appearance so it is easy to see why sick people were sometimes mistaken for changelings. This was unfortunate because of the belief that changelings would disappear if burnt and the stolen individual would then be returned. There is a story about a man who thought a changeling had been left in the place of his dearly loved wife. He picked her up and threw her on the fire. She burnt to death. The man was overcome with sorrow and committed suicide. Black (typhus) fever changed the appearance of its victims to such an extent that their relatives did not recognise them. It is very likely that a few black fever victims were suspected of being changelings and burnt to death.

Mothers were advised never to leave a baby sleeping alone beside the fire without leaving the fire irons across the cradle. Iron was thought to offer protection against fairies.

What happened to the fairies? Belief in them is not as common as in the past. People say that fairies have left Ireland. There are many explanations offered for their disappearance. Some say they became disgusted by human behaviour and went into the walls at Killyleagh, County Down; others say the fairies from the north of Ireland fought those from the south and they annihilated each other. Another explanation is that they blew away in the "big wind" of 1839, the hurricane that caused widespread damage throughout Ireland.

Ireland also has legends about giants. Finn McCool is one of the most famous of these. He is supposed to have been very bad-tempered and hated a giant who lived on the west coast of Scotland. According to folklore he lost his temper one day with the Scottish giant, bent down and picked up a handful of earth to throw at his enemy. He missed, the earth fell into the sea and formed the Isle of Man while the hole left behind filled up with water and turned into Lough Neagh, the largest lake in these islands.

The Giant's Causeway on the north Antrim coast is also said to be the result of Finn McCool's activities. The two giants decided to have a battle but neither would agree to let the other set foot in his territory. They then decided each to build a roadway across the sea from the north Irish coast to the isle of Staffa in the Hebrides. Finn died before the causeway was finished and the Scots giant ceased work after an impressive beginning at Fingal's cave. Finn left one of his boots behind and that has turned to stone.

Finn McCool's boot, Giant's Causeway, County Antrim

In Ireland today few people admit to believing in fairies, leprechauns or giants. However, many people are fearful of the supernatural. The type of feeling commonly expressed is: "I do not believe in fairies but I will not interfere with that fairy thorn just in case it could cause trouble!"

9

Cures and Customs

Life must have been very frightening in the past because people did not have the benefit of modern, scientific knowledge. Animals, people and crops could suddenly sicken and die without apparent reason. The all-important weather could turn nasty and destroy a crop. In the past, however, people lived very much closer to nature than they do today. They were constantly on the lookout for signs that could be used to foretell the future. This gave rise both to superstitions and to ideas, based on observation, that were useful. Superstitions, ideas and observations from the past are preserved in folklore. Take the following well-known rhyme:

> Red sky at night
> Shepherd's delight;
> Red sky in the morning
> Shepherd's warning.

In Ireland it is amazing how frequently good weather follows an evening during which the sky was red and how frequently a day of bad weather is preceded by a red sky in the morning.

People used to take careful note of the first butterfly they spotted in the year. A brown butterfly was said to mean that the individual would eat brown bread for the remainder of the year. Brown bread was eaten by people who were not wealthy so the brown butterfly was a sign of poor crops and poverty. On the other hand a white butterfly denoted white bread and wealth. People in Ireland today are becoming increasingly health-conscious so that attitudes to brown and white bread have changed. Brown bread, on account of its higher fibre content, is believed to be better than white. Butterflies hatch at different times of the year, depending on temperature, so it could very well be that when the conditions cause white butterflies to hatch first they will also be good for growing crops.

Many people believed that butterflies were the souls of the dead. There is a story of a little girl whose grandfather had just died. A butterfly flew into the house and she chased after it. Her grandmother was very cross and scolded her, saying that she should let her grandfather rest in peace. The little girl cried for the rest of the day because she loved her grandfather and was upset to think that she had disturbed him.

There is an old saying regarding magpies:

> One for sorrow;
> Two for joy.

Seagoing fishermen used to look carefully for magpies. If the weather is going to be poor, one magpie from each breeding pair remains on the nest while the other forages for food, so the old rhyme is based on observation. In the past people thought that the bad luck foretold by the sight of a solitary magpie could be averted by greeting it with the words: "Good morning, Mr Magpie."

When the rooks build their nests high in the trees that is a sign of a good summer. Frogs lay their eggs in the centre of the pond, if the weather is going to be warm, and at the edge, if it is going to be cold. A plentiful supply of haws and rose-hips in autumn means that the winter is going to be very cold.

There is an old saying about bees:

> A swarm of bees in May
> Is worth a load of hay.
> A swarm of bees in June
> Is worth a silver spoon.
> A swarm of bees in July
> Is not worth a fly.

In other words, if the weather is sufficiently good to enable bees to pollinate plants early in the year and then to reproduce and swarm, the harvest will be good. If the bees are not able to swarm until later in the year then the crops will be poor.

Old folk cures are also interesting. In the days before penicillin was discovered a piece of mouldy bread was always kept in a safe place about the house. People knew it was excellent for curing festered wounds and suppurating sores. While working in the laboratories of St Mary's Hospital in Paddington, Sir Alexander Fleming discovered that penicillin is a very common mould The practice of DIY antibiotics is very old: the ancient Chinese used mouldy bread to cure sores on the feet.

There is a story about a young boy who went to work in a cobbler's shop as an apprentice. He was asked to tidy the shop as his first job and left alone. The boy brushed the floor then spied all the cobwebs hanging from the ceiling. He thought they looked very dirty so used the brush to knock them down and to sweep gently around the ceiling. When the cobbler returned he flew into a rage and beat the boy around the head for being so stupid. The cobwebs were used to staunch bleeding. They were wrapped around any cut the cobbler might happen to inflict upon himself with his sharp instruments. He told the unfortunate boy he would be held directly responsible if anyone on the premises bled to death before the spiders had time to renew their webs. Needless to say the boy never touched another spider's web.

Pains caused by rheumatism were cured by being rubbed with garlic, which was also thought good for colds and coughs. Garlic was also believed to be good for the blood and for heart complaints. Today doctors have discovered that garlic keeps blood from clotting too quickly and it reduces cholesterol levels. Garlic was also used for skin complaints. A cat, called Jason, who lived in the Folk and Transport Museum at Cultra was pampered by the shop assistants and some of the attendants at the museum. He had a tendency to develop skin complaints and was often taken to the vet to be given many expensive injections. In spite of all the care and attention lavished upon him his skin continued to be troublesome. Then one day someone decided to try the old folk cure, garlic, on Jason's sores. The contents of a garlic capsule were squeezed over Jason's sores three times each day. They healed rapidly.

Garlic was a very common crop in Ireland until about the time of the First World War. It was used as a general cure-all. Slices of garlic placed in the shoes against the soles of the feet was a cure for whooping-cough. This sounds ludicrous but it is a fact that garlic placed against the soles of the feet is smelt on the breath within fifteen minutes.

Feverfew was used to cure the pain of rheumatism and headaches. Two or three leaves from the plant were eaten each day in a sandwich, often with remarkably good results. Modern research has shown that feverfew is an effective treatment for these conditions.

Digitalis, the drug found in foxgloves, is an old cure for heart disease that is still in use today. Foxgloves are very poisonous so they must never be eaten without supervision by a doctor.

Ivy was used as a cure for corns. It was tied around the sore toe and left on for several days. Some people used to boil ivy leaves in water and use the water to wash the corns before rubbing them with the leaves. People believed that if they bound their heads in ivy they could drink as much alcohol as they wanted without becoming drunk!

In the past many people were thought to have the ability to charm disease away. An old lady, now dead, who lived in Aghalee was said to have a charm for shingles. A friend of mine described a visit to her. She gave him a flannel belt, with herbs inside, to wear next to his skin, made the Sign of the Cross over his head and muttered something strange about him. She refused any payment, saying that the ability to cure came from God and could not be exchanged for money. Payment would cause her powers to disappear. My friend was very impressed and came home feeling he was bound to be better soon. Unfortunately he has sensitive skin and the flannel irritated it causing him to itch. He removed the belt, saying he would just let the shingles run their natural course! The

"We couldn't possibly be drunk—our heads are bound with ivy."

cure was just as bad as the disease!

I once met an old woman whose left leg had been burnt by a fire several years before. The leg appeared swollen, red and sore, and caused her a lot of discomfort. Doctors seemed unable to prescribe anything to help. Eventually she heard of an old pishogue, or wise woman, who lived near Coalisland and who was said to have a cure for "bad legs." She went to see her. The pishogue invited her in and sat and chatted for some time. Eventually she said, "I think I can do something for your leg." She made the Sign of the Cross over the old woman's head and then made other strange signs around about her. She muttered something incomprehensible and said a prayer. Immediately the leg felt a lot better. In time the swelling disappeared and the red mark faded.

Charms were handed down from one generation to the next and there is no doubt that some, at least, were effective. Many probably had the same type of effect as doctors' placebos: sheer belief in them made them work.

Throughout Ireland there are places such as the Struel Wells near Downpatrick and the stream beside St Brigid's Shrine at Faughart near Dundalk, which are believed to have curative powers. There are four wells at Struel, one for drinking, two for washing the body and, most famous, the one specifically for eye-complaints. There are many interesting legends explaining how they obtained their curative powers in the first place. One story suggests that St Patrick slept in a cave with his head resting against a rock and spring water sprayed his beard and clothes. Ordinary mortals would doubtless have cursed the water but Patrick was a saint so he blessed it, giving it curative powers.

The stream associated with St Brigid's Shrine at Faughart

Pieces of cloth left by pilgrims hoping for a cure near St Brigid's Shrine, Faughart, County Louth

Struel Well near Downpatrick, County Down

is interesting. It comes rushing down the mountain side and different parts of it are associated with different parts of the body. People visiting the stream seeking a cure are expected to leave some personal possession behind. The general feeling is that if one expects to take something away, in the form of a cure, some sort of symbol should be left in return. Stockings, handkerchiefs, socks and other small items of clothing, belonging to the pilgrims, are tied to sticks, or anything else that is suitable, and left fluttering in the breeze. The same practice can be found at Doon Well in Donegal. The holy places associated with these cures are not visited as frequently as they were in the past but some people still go because they still believe.

It would appear many of the old folk cures were useful. They are not as strong as modern drugs and take a longer time to work but usually have fewer side effects. There is renewed and steadily increasing interest in them and many are gaining a respectable place in conjunction with modern medicine.

10

The Whole Year Round

Each winter the earth grows cold and plants stop growing. Deciduous trees lose their leaves and herbaceous plants appear dead. Then gradually winter turns into spring and life appears renewed. Primitive people did not have the knowledge to understand the seasons. Each autumn they felt that perhaps the sun had disappeared for good. This belief led to superstitions and customs, some of which persist to the present day, incorporated in our Christian festivals such as Christmas and Easter.

To begin with, evergreen plants were looked upon as something very special: they could survive the winter without losing their leaves. They never appeared dead so they came to symbolise everlasting life and were used as decorations at the ancient pagan festivals. Their presence demonstrated that winter does not necessarily result in death, that the sun would return in the spring bringing light, warmth and growth. When Jesus, The Light of the World, was born, His birthday came to be associated with the pagan feasts of the winter solstice. Pagan people found it easier to go on celebrating at the same period as they had always done—so the pagan feast became Christmas.

Lane, Ballybracken, Co Antrim. The seasonal changes in deciduous
trees and other plants led to fertility rites.

CHRISTMAS

The eastern church believed that Jesus was born on the sixth of January so they celebrated Christmas at a different time from the western church. During the fifth century all the churches, except the Armenian, decided to extend the festivities until the sixth of January so that the celebration would also honour the baptism of Christ and the visit of the Three Wise Men. This is the origin of the Twelve Days of Christmas. In Ireland, even two generations ago, only the rich gave each other Christmas presents. Country people would have expected a Christmas "box" from their grocer. The box would have held food and perhaps a calendar.

The decoration of houses with holly and ivy as a symbol of everlasting life is a custom that survives from the past, so is the lighting of the Christmas or Yule candle on Christmas Eve. A Yule candle was placed in the window as a symbol of hospitality to remember the circumstances

"I wonder what I should give
Daisy to eat for Christmas?"

of Christ's birth. The door of the house might be left open for the same reason. Yule candles were often coloured and each district appeared to have its own taste in colour. At the present time people tend to leave their curtains open at Christmas so that the light from their living-rooms shines out. Christmas trees, with electric fairy lights replacing candles, are commonplace.

Christmas Day was marked by church services and by special meals. Many a poor family had their only meat dish of the year on Christmas Day. There is an old saying in County Down: "Glory be to Christmas, the day we get the beef." In fact the "beef" was usually goose. Traditionally animals were also given extra food on Christmas Day.

THE MUMMERS

In Ireland the big event of midwinter was the visit of the mummers. It has been suggested that mumming came from a spring ceremony of Graeco-Oriental pagan origin and that the strength of feeling in Ireland about Christmas caused the custom to be moved from spring to midwinter. Mummers were a group of between eight and sixteen young men. They went from house to house performing a play based on an ancient fertility rite, in which death and coming back from the dead symbolised the death of life in winter and the rebirth that happens every spring. The mummers' play began with the actors' entrance. This was followed by some sort of fight between the two principal characters, usually St Patrick and St George, resulting in the death of one of them. Many of the plays had a Turk in them because Turks fought the Crusaders. The play came to an end when a doctor revived the warrior who had been killed. This was followed by the entrance of a number of colourful characters such as clowns, dancers and musicians whose main job was to collect money. Devil Doubt was a great favourite. He had a sweeping brush, a hat to collect the money and a very specific rhyme:

> Here I am, little Devil Doubt.
> If yous don't give me money
> I'll sweep yous all out!

Mummers usually wore long white shirts decorated with coloured ribbons to make them look feathered. Some of the characters had their faces blackened, others carried cudgels, or swords and shields made of wood. Some characters wore tall hats made of paper or straw. The troupes were very conscious of territorial rights. If one group met another working on disputed territory they fought until one lot became exhausted and retired. The other group continued mumming. The Armagh Rhymers are now the best-known group of mummers. They make frequent appearances at the Ulster Folk and Transport Museum. One of the Rhymers, Dara Vallely, says that the plays frequently have a curative effect on people who are mentally disturbed. He described a visit to Gilford in County Down. A young autistic boy was a member of the audience. The boy was completely withdrawn and never spoke. He became very excited by the noise and the colour of the play. He began talking to his teacher and members of his class. When he went home he astonished his mother by saying, "Mum, will you give me a banana?"

HUNTING THE WREN

The hunting of the wren on 26 December may also have come from Graeco-Oriental practice. Bands of youths would hunt for a wren and kill it. Then, dressed as fools or as women or in suits made from straw with straw masks, they formed a noisy procession and demanded money to bury the wren. The bird was carried on a decorated wooden tray or on a holly bush. In more recent times a toy bird was used instead of a dead one and sometimes a bird was not used at all. An interesting reason for killing wrens is suggested by Irish folklore. Apparently Irish soldiers decided to mount a surprise attack on Cromwell and his army. Under the cover of darkness they managed to draw near to Cromwell and had nearly surrounded him when wrens, perched on the drums of Cromwell's troops, pecked at them with their beaks. They made such a noise that Cromwell and his army awoke, fell upon the Irish and slaughtered them. Wrens are killed on St Stephen's Day, that is, 26 December, as revenge.

The wrenboys might also perform a mumming play. The leader, carrying the dead wren in its holly bush, would call for space to act the play:

> Room, room brave gallant boys,
> Come give us room to rhyme!
> We've come to show activity
> Upon this Christmas time:
> Acts of young and acts of age—
> The like was never acted on the stage.
> If you don't believe what I say
> Enter in Sir Patrick and clear the way.

The Armagh Rhymers replace the dead wren with a brown potato!

New Year's Day

New Year's Day was a time for preserving the luck of the household. There was a belief that happiness and prosperity depended on the first person to enter the house on New Year's Day. A dark-haired man was thought to be lucky as a "first-footer." Women were thought to be unlucky, especially if they had red hair. Marie Ward, who lives near Dromore, County Down, has described how her father made wisps from part of the last sheaf cut at the harvest. The stalks of the grain were plaited, leaving the grain heads hanging. The stalk ends were held in place by brightly coloured ribbons tied into a bow. Every New Year's Eve, Marie's father sent her to Belfast with a wisp to his sister's house in one of the streets off the Lisburn Road. Marie had to find a dark-haired man to carry the wisp and a lump of coal into the house before she could enter.

There is a tradition in some streets in Belfast which continues to this day. According to Lil McCusken, who used to live in East Belfast, at midnight on New Year's Eve all the doors in the street open and people shout greetings, offer each other drinks and a neighbour walks a donkey around the houses. A donkey has a mark on its back that resembles a cross. Tradition says that Jesus put that mark there after riding on a donkey on Palm Sunday. The cross gives protection against evil. When Lil moved to the Lisburn Road area she says she missed the crack on New Year's Eve because people in her new neighbourhood do not carry on the old custom. She says it is still celebrated in her old street.

St Brigid's Day

Traditionally in rural Ireland the first day of February, St Brigid's Day, was looked upon as the first day of spring. The saint was supposed to have placed her foot in the water on her feast-day and caused the weather to begin to become warm. Saints are commonly believed to return to earth for their festive day so doors were left on the latch so that the house could be entered easily. In some districts dandelions are called St Brigid's flower because they are usually the first flowers to appear after her feast. On St Brigid's Eve children pulled rushes (they were never cut) and left them in a bundle outside the house. A special meal was prepared, usually consisting of pancakes or currant bread. Then a ceremony followed. This varied considerably from one neighbourhood to another. In some places a member of the family, usually a daughter, was sent out to represent the saint. She returned with the

St Brigid's Shrine,
Faughart, County
Louth

rushes and was made welcome. The family used the rushes to make St Brigid crosses. In other places the crosses were made before the meal, sprinkled with holy water and placed under each dish. Once the crosses were made they were blessed by the local priest or sprinkled with holy water or taken to mass. They were then placed over the door, usually by the third day after the feast, in the hope that the family would have a plentiful supply of food for the following twelve months. Sometimes St Brigid crosses were placed under the thatch or in the byre to protect the house and livestock from fire and disease.

St Patrick's Day

St Patrick's Day has a curious lack of traditional customs although patriotic Irish wear shamrocks. St Brigid encouraged the weather to become warmer but it was St Patrick who turned the "warm side of the stone upper-

St Patrick's grave,
Downpatrick

most." Farmers still like to have their potato crop in the ground before St Patrick's Day. The great "movable" religious festivals of the church—Easter, Ascension Day and Whitsun—come after St Patrick's Day. Their dates are determined by the day on which Easter falls, which is reckoned as the first Sunday after the first full moon after the vernal equinox.

SHROVE TUESDAY

Shrove Tuesday was never one of the great festivals in Ireland. It is the last day before the beginning of Lent so it was looked upon as a "great day for weddings." Weddings were forbidden during Lent. Lent is traditionally a time of penance. Today people still give up things, such as chocolates, alcohol, tobacco and meat, for Lent. Shrove Tuesday is a day when it is customary to have a few treats, to indulge the body, before the sacrifices of Lent. Pancakes are still made as a treat on that day. It was thought, too, to be a good day for playing tricks on children, courting couples and unmarried people. Children could be sent to a neighbour's house to ask for the loan of a "pancake sieve" and might innocently visit several houses before discovering the trick. They could also be sent next door to ask for "the oil of a hazel," that is, a good beating.

EASTER

Easter begins on Good Friday because that is the day of the Crucifixion. In Ireland it was thought to be the luckiest day to begin sowing corn, although ploughing and the use of iron implements were avoided. Easter Sunday, marking the end of Lent, had a gay atmosphere. In Ireland it was customary to wear an item of new clothing on Easter Sunday. As children my sister and I always had a

new summer outfit to wear to church on Easter Sunday.
There were times when we stood shivering in our new,
flimsy clothing during cold March gales. When we asked
our mother why we could not be sensible and wear our
old, winter coats she replied that she did not really know.
She supposed it would be unlucky to do so. I remember
one particularly cold Easter when my sister and I felt we
would be lucky not to catch pneumonia!

Another old custom was to get up early in the morning
to "see the sun dance." Tradition says that Christ rose
from the dead at dawn on Easter Sunday and that the sun
danced for joy. In remembrance the light from the sun
was reflected on a silver spoon and allowed to dance on
the wall. Sometimes a saucer of water was used instead.
My grandfather used a saucer of water and when he saw
my amazement at the reflections dancing on the wall he
took out his silver hunter's watch and swung it from its
chain so that its reflection also danced on the wall. When
I laughed and laughed he told me to remember that it was
just an old-fashioned custom with a serious thought
behind it. He also said that no matter how dull and wet
the weather was on Easter morning it was always possible
to obtain a reflection of the dancing sun upon the wall.

In pagan times an egg was looked upon as an emblem
of fertility, a symbol of the renewal of life. The early
Christian church used eggs as a symbol of the Resurrection.
Traditionally eggs were eaten at Easter. In more recent
times it would appear that chocolate eggs are eaten on
Easter Sunday and hard-boiled ones on Easter Monday.
Children rolled hard-boiled eggs along the grass until
they broke. Then they ate them. The hard-boiled eggs
were usually brightly coloured by being boiled with a dye.
Sometimes patterns were made on the shells. The egg

may have been wrapped in a piece of another plant, such as an onion skin, so that the part that was covered remained white. Sometimes the child's initials were rubbed on the egg with a tallow candle. The dye did not have any effect on the place where the tallow had been. The shells were often saved to decorate the May bush in the May Day festivities. My mother remembered as a child going to Bellevue which was then on the outskirts of Belfast on Easter Monday and rolling her egg down the hill. Her father told her to roll her egg down a hill as the Cross had stood on a hill's top. Mother's egg was dyed by boiling it in a pot with tea leaves. Sometimes the family gathered whin flowers and boiled the eggs with them and a teaspoonful of salt. Tea gave a brown dye while whin turned them yellow.

WHITSUN

Whitsun is the seventh Sunday after Easter. It marks the coming of the Holy Spirit and the end of the Easter season. Strangely, in Ireland, it was thought to be a very unlucky day. People born on Whitsun were thought likely to have the evil eye or to be fated to grow up and commit murder. A chicken was sometimes killed in the hands of a Whitsun child to serve as a substitute for a human life thus preventing the murder. Fairies and evil spirits were thought to be around at Whitsun so people were advised not to fall asleep in the open in case they were taken by the fairies. People were also advised not to cross water or to go to sea because the souls of those who had drowned would attempt to run away with anyone who went near them. Whitsun does not appear to have had associations with evil in Britain and it is difficult to say why it should do so in Ireland, especially as the coming of the Holy Ghost was a joyful Christian event.

May Day, the festival of *Bealtaine*

The Gaelic name for the month of May is *Bealtaine*. The festival of Bealtaine was celebrated on the first of May. This was the first day of summer and a holiday. The crops were safely in the ground and people had a brief break before turf-cutting and haymaking began. It was a day of gatherings and of fairs. A dish of stirabout (porridge) was always served on that day because it showed that the woman of the house was a good, thrifty housewife. She had made her supply of corn last. Even those who were short of corn tried to save some for May Day.

Bealtaine is one of the few pagan festivals that has not been absorbed into the Christian calendar. Fairies and witches were believed to have great power for evil on that day. Fairies were supposed to travel in groups from place to place, holding feasts and dances in raths. (Raths were made by prehistoric man. They were raised areas used as defensive positions for houses or as places where cattle would be safe.) Sometimes fairies wanted human company so they stole adults and children. Changelings were left in their place. Fairies were also thought to contaminate food on May Eve. They stole the real food away at night and left poisonous pieces of turf disguised to look like food behind.

Any food left over from May Eve was not eaten. It was buried in the garden or thrown over the townland's boundary for the dogs. Bonfires were lit, usually on the top of hills, and men and women jumped over the flames and later drove their cattle through the smouldering ashes as protection against evil and to increase fertility. Milk cows were thought to be in need of special protection against evil. Bunches of primroses were tied to cows' tails because evil spirits were thought to be unable to touch anything guarded by them. Rowan trees were also thought to protect against evil so sprigs of rowan were hung outside the byre door or placed on the milking vessel or hung from the cow's horns.

Witches had the power, especially at Bealtaine, to turn themselves into hares. They could then suck milk from the cows and charm a year's supply of butter away. They also gathered dew from the fields where the cows grazed by lifting it into a bucket or sheet. This cast a spell so that the milk belonged to the witch rather than the farmer.

The fire symbolises the heart of the house. On May Day witches were thought to be anxious to steal fire. As a result a number of customs arose. In some places it was thought to be unlucky to kindle a fire on May Day. In other places it was considered unlucky to be the first house to show smoke and so on May morning the cattle were milked and the byre swept clean before the fire was lit. In other areas nobody lit a fire until smoke was seen rising from the priest's chimney.

In the past the manure heap was regarded as an important symbol of fertility. Rowan branches were placed on it to protect it from evil. In the days before artificial fertilisers the manure heap was vital to ensure the growth of crops so it was sensible to protect it. Sometimes whin bushes were placed on the manure heap instead of rowan.

On May Day too people collected flowers and scattered them along window sills, on thresholds and sometimes on house roofs. My next-door neighbour, who is 88 years of age, remembers that, as a girl living in Banbridge, she collected marsh marigolds and brought them into the house in Dromore Street for her mother. At that time, in country districts around Banbridge, people tied marsh marigolds in bunches and hung them from the door

"Guess why I have primroses tied to my tail!"

knocker of their houses to keep the fairies away. In other parts of the country ragwort was used. A child in Dromore told me that her father always singed the shape of a cross on her pony's back on May Eve. He used a match to do so. The child did not know why her father did this but supposed the Sign of the Cross was a protection against evil. She could not think of any reason for having to protect horses against evil on May Day.

In Belfast an old tradition was observed every May Day. Young boys and girls, both Protestant and Catholic, used to go and collect yarrow from the Bog Meadows, the common between the Lisburn and the Falls Roads. This was reported in the *Northern Whig* newspaper. Unfortunately, according to the *Whig*, sectarian violence erupted in what had been a happy custom based on old fertility rites so that it died out by the 1880s.

Another interesting custom, the choosing of the Queen of the May, was enacted by small girls. This custom, like that of mumming, was very territorial. If two rival groups met they fought. The May Queen was usually fairly athletic and had to be able to obtain the necessary costume. She dressed up in crêpe paper, or lace curtains, donned a crown and carried the decorated shaft of a brush. Valerie Hall remembers being a May Queen in the Donegall Pass area of Belfast in the mid-1950s and her mother sitting up late at night using a sewing machine and crêpe paper to make a costume, then decorating the brush-shaft. Valerie says the brush-shaft was very important and had to be carried horizontally. I remember seeing a May Queen about the same period of time on the Castlereagh Road near the old Castle Cinema, which was at the junction between the Castlereagh Road and Clara Street. She was dressed in lace curtains with hundreds of shining beads hanging around her neck. The little girls around her sang:

Our wee Queen can birl her leg,
Birl her leg, birl her leg;
Our wee Queen can birl her leg
On a cold and frosty morning.

The little queen, using a circular movement, kicked her right leg as high in the air as she could and back down again, while her courtiers sang. The courtiers collected money which was divided out fairly among members of the group. This chance of collecting money was the main cause of the trouble between the rival queens.

May is the month of Mary, Mother of Jesus. On May Eve she is thought to return to earth and walk around the countryside. In the past people scattered bluebells and marsh marigolds on the ground so she could walk on them. If they appeared flattened next day it was said that she had passed the house. Dancing around a maypole is an English tradition. It was not usual in Ireland. There is a maypole in Holywood, County Down. I remember holding a coloured ribbon in my hand and dancing around it as a child. Strangers, like me, were made very welcome and a very nice gentleman directed the dancing in a kindly, humorous fashion so we knew what to do. As we danced round and round the maypole the ribbons became shorter and shorter as they became wrapped around the pole. Eventually dancing became impossible because everyone was holding a short piece of ribbon against the pole. Everyone laughed and the dancing was reversed so that the pole was unwrapped. This custom is continued in Holywood to the present day.

MIDSUMMER DAY

The birthday of St John the Baptist is celebrated on Midsummer Day. The feast was marked by lighting bonfires on hilltops. Fires were also lit in front of byre doors and at country crossroads. People danced to music supplied by a fiddler and the custom of leaping the flames was common. Sometimes guns were fired into the air to frighten evil spirits. The Ulster Folk and Transport Museum celebrate St John's Eve each year by organising special events and lighting a bonfire in the grounds.

THE TWELFTH

The celebrations of 12 July commemorate William III's victory at the battle of the Boyne in 1690. They are sectarian and Protestant in nature, ignoring the historical fact that the Pope was an unofficial supporter of King William! Bonfires are lit in Protestant areas on the eleventh night, people may dance around them although they are more likely to sit or stand nearby drinking, singing sectarian songs and cracking. Strangers visiting a bonfire are treated in a friendly, hospitable manner and the crack is usually good. I know many Catholics who join their Protestant friends for the eleventh night celebrations and the marches held on the following day. They really enjoy themselves!

Lambeg Drum, Sandy Row,
Eleventh night, Belfast, 1990

Crowd watching bonfire,
Eleventh night, Belfast, 1990

The Twelfth is essentially the day of the march of members of the Orange Order. They carry banners and are accompanied by bands so that it is one of the most colourful and festive days in the calendar in Northern Ireland. 12 July may be contrasted with 15 August, the feast of the Assumption of the Virgin Mary, which, for Ulster Catholics, is an important feast-day with religious services and outings and, like the Twelfth, an opportunity to display sectarian emblems.

LAMMAS

Lammas Day was celebrated on either the last Sunday in July or the first Sunday in August. The name "Lammas," as we saw in chapter five, is derived from Lughnasa, meaning August and thus the start of harvest. Lughnasa is maned after the ancient pagan god of harvest, Lugh, who was Cuchulain's father. At harvest time young people were permitted to go together unchaperoned. Another

Auld Lammas Fair, Ballycastle, County Antrim

ancient god, called Pilgra, is also celebrated at this time so young people were sent on pilgrimages. It is traditional to visit the holy well at Belcoo, County Fermanagh; there is also the great annual pilgrimage to Croagh Patrick in which on the last Sunday in July several thousand people climb barefoot the County Mayo mountain. However, for most people the great event was the pilgrimage to gather bilberries or whortleberries. The Gaelic name for the bilberry is *fraochán* and so the day is often called Fraughan Sunday. Many a man met his wife for the first time while on an unchaperoned pilgrimage to gather bilberries.

HARVEST

September and October were the busiest months for farmers. Friends, neighbours and paid labourers banded together to help each other bring in the harvest before the invention of machines. They moved from farm to farm until the work was done. There was usually a gay and boisterous atmosphere because people were together for a long period of time and there was a mixing of old and young of both sexes.

One of the most interesting events in the harvest was the cutting of the last sheaf, which was also called the "hare" or the *cailleach*. The women, who usually acted as binders, plaited the last small amount of growing corn and tied its top with a few straws. Reapers and binders then danced around the hare until someone called out, "Cut her down." The reapers and sometimes the women as well marked out a distance of approximately six yards and one by one threw their hooks at the hare in an attempt to sever it with a single stroke. When the hare was cut it could be hung up in the house or the barn to bring luck with the following harvest. Sometimes it was plaited into wisps which were hung in the barn or given away on New Year's Eve. The hare could also serve as decoration in the local church harvest festival.

Once the harvest was gathered the workers were treated to a special meal, sometimes called the churn. After the churn there was a barn dance. This took place at each farm as the harvest was completed so people had a hectic social life during harvest time.

HALLOWE'EN

Hallowe'en marked the end of the farming year and the beginning of winter so it was a very important festival. According to folklore the supernatural world has then the greatest power to influence the life of humans. As a child I always dressed up at Hallowe'en and went outside with my friends to frighten ghosts away. Sometimes we pretended we were ghosts and played a game described as "thunder and lightning," in other words we knocked on doors like thunder and ran away like lightning. We hoped that people answering the door would think that a ghost had visited the house!

We had a very cross neighbour who objected to our playing street games outside his house. When we played ball games he used to come and take our ball. We felt this was very unfair because we were always careful to confine the ball to the street and keep it out of the gardens. We got our revenge at Hallowe'en. Emboldened by our disguises we repeatedly knocked upon his door and ran away. The gentleman's name was Mr Hoey so we stood outside his house and shouted:

Old Hoey
Sat on his po-ey

as well as anything else rude that came to mind.

We enjoyed making a bonfire and dancing around it. We always had fireworks and took particular delight in letting off "bangers." Once we lit a banger and threw it into Old Hoey's house through the letter-box. We were very repentant when we realised how dangerous our action was. Fireworks were forbidden after 1969 when the army was called into Northern Ireland. The troops decided that our much-loved bangers sounded like gunfire and they found the noise alarming. After that time fireworks were confined to official displays organised by such bodies as district councils.

We believed that the dead walked around on Hallowe'en night and that they could take revenge on the living. We were warned never to look behind us if we heard footsteps because if we caught the eye of the dead we ourselves would surely die. I do not think we took that threat seriously because we definitely looked behind us to see if Old Hoey was chasing us. Sometimes he was!

Children still dress up at Hallowe'en; they still make lanterns out of turnips and play practical jokes. A favourite trick today appears to be to remove garden gates and hide them somewhere in the garden.

Calendar customs still form an integral part of life in Ireland although in the North many people stopped observing the old traditions during the Second World War. The blackout, introduced to give protection from German bombers, made it inadvisable to light bonfires at the appropriate times during the year. People were too busy with the war effort to have time to observe all but the most important festivals. Increasing scientific knowledge means there is less superstition so there is no real reason, in that sense, for carrying on the old traditions.

However, many families enjoy carrying out the old customs. It can be fun, gives a sense of unity and reminds us that there is more to life than materialism.

There are remarkable differences in the observance of traditional customs in different areas. Let us rejoice in those variations. We live in a time when in so many ways life is becoming uniform throughout the world. The architecture of tourist resorts is so universal that it is almost impossible to guess from its appearance where a strange hotel room is. Our best hope for the future is to keep a sense of our identity by being proud of our local traditions and customs and by keeping them alive. Let us hope that in the future people will preserve at least some of the local traditionsand customs I have described because they make us interesting and make us who we are. Or to put it another way: we are our past.

Further Reading

Antrim and District Historical Society, *Dear Uncle, Immigrant Letters from Antrim to the USA*, 1989.

Bell, Jonathan and Mervyn Watson, *Farming in Ulster*, Belfast, 1988.

— and Doreen McBride, Ulster Farm and Food, (Activity Pack), Belfast, 1989.

Dallat, Cahal and Faith Gibson, *Rooms of Time*, Belfast, 1988.

Danaher, Kevin, *The Hearth and Stool and All!*, Cork, *1985*.

Evans, E Estyn, *Irish Folk Ways*, London, 1957.

Glassie, Henry, *Irish Folk History*, Dublin, 1982.

Lenihan, Edmund, *In Search of Biddy Early*, Cork, 1987.

Logan, Patrick, *Irish Country Cures*, Belfast, 1981.

McBride, Doreen, *What They Did with Plants*, Banbridge, 1991.

—, *Ulster Folk and Transport Museum Activity Guide,* London, 1989.

Scott, Michael, ed., *An Irish Herbal*, London, 1986.

Sharkey, Olive, *Old Days, Old Ways*, Dublin, 1985.

Wilde, Lady, *Quaint Irish Customs and Superstitions*, Cork, 1988.

Yeats, WB, ed., *Irish Fairy and Other Folk Tales*, London.

Index